A PLETHORA OF SCENIC SPLENDOURS

A Remark on the Journey to Singapore and Malaysia

層層山水秀

by Living Buddha Lian-Sheng
Translated by Yuan Zheng Tang of True
Buddha School（Singapore）

First Published in 1995
Lian Kuei Publishing House
Taipei, Taiwan, Republic of China

Distributed in Republic of China by

© Lian Kuei Publishing House, Taiwan 1995
P.O. BOX 26-765 TAIPEI TAIWAN R.O.C.

Printed in Taiwan, Republic of China

ISBN 957 − 8926 − 10 − 3

Price : US$ 10.00

PREFACE

With a view to propagating the dharma, I made a trip to Singapore and Malaysia from December 1992 to January 1993.

This book entitled " A plethora of scenic splendours" gives an account on what I have seen and heard during my stint. I would like to dedicate it to:

All the True Buddha disciples,
All the truth seekers,
All the true Buddhists,
and all the friends of the same faith.

This is the 104th book written by me. It closely reflects my propagating journeys.

The "supposedly short" tour turned out to be very exciting. Unlike the conventional sight-seeing, I had to bear the brunt of lashings, wage a war, face a revolution, and finally conclude them to be just illusions.

Discerning readers must use their wisdom to analyze what is right and what is wrong without jumping to conclusions.

As the book stresses on the truthfulness , it has an absolute power in it regardless of what yardstick you may want to use in judging it.

You may be a little puzzled after reading the book; or see the traditional Buddhist organizations in a different light. Some of you may even disagree with my views, albeit

you can't stop me from writing this book.

Neither do I wish to brag about my wisdom, nor do I pretend to be humble, I just write what I have to say!

I admit my work to be logical; and yet I could be carried away by my emotion. It flows naturally like an ocean, a stream, a river or a lake. It is as clear and thorough as the morning sun. It is like the flowers in the garden that blossom suddenly. I may claim that immediately after touring the destinations, i.e. Singapore and Malaysia (East and West), the articles were completed once my emotion started to wane.

A plethora of scenic splendours, among the high-rise building and passing crowd, I saw the Bodhi tree which is as serene as ever, I saw the primitive forest, and undulated mountains, and I admire the greatness of nature.

"Why did you go to Singapore and Malaysia ?" I am asked. My answer, "My disciples there invited me, so I went." It is as simple as that. I have many disciples in these countries who wished that their grandmaster could visit them like their relatives so that they can receive the benevolence of the Buddhas and Bodhisattvas.

Under such adverse conditions as oppression from the traditional schools and unfair treatment , the disciples from Singapore and Malaysia show their confidence. They do not mourn the past; nor worry about the future, instead they glow with enthusiasm and radiating vigour. They say that :"As long as the grandmaster is here, everything is fine and considered perfect."

What is dharma-propagation ?

It surely is "life".

It is also a "cultivation".

It is a special kind of "experience".

It is the practical usage of dharma.

4

The most important of all:

"It is a pure and profound understanding of the deep meditation."

I sincerely hope the incessant power of this book will light up the souls of all mankind, and render them to be simple, bright and clear.

May 1993
Sheng-Yen Lu
True Buddha Tantric Garden
17102 NE 40th CT
Redmond, WA 98052 U.S.A.

CONTENTS

6

Sanskrit words and Moon disc appearing on top of the head

It is said that Master Lu Sheng-Yen achieves his great reputation through constant displaying of his mystic power.

The religious fraternity takes great delight in talking about this. It causes a commotion. As a result his photographs always appear on the cover of magazines, and he becomes the headline of many influential newspapers.

For a religious practitioner, his experience belongs to a rare species.

In the wee hours of December 15, 1992, master Lu Sheng-Yen, accompanied by Guru Lian Xiang, Guru Chang Ren, and Guru Lian Man arrived at the Singapore Changi International Airport.

In the past, wherever Master Lu Sheng Yan went, he was the focal point, and created news.

Many thousands came to welcome him,
Many hundreds came to garland him,
Many lined the airport to chant the heart mantra
    of Living Buddha Lian Sheng,
All of them knelt and bowed to him.

This snap short at the airport is considered

nothing unusual.

In fact, I have come to realise that I am as common as anybody else. I have my views and my feelings.

I am the leading cast in a religious school that advocates personal cultivation. I founded the school. As a founder, I must have perseverance, unsurpassed tolerance, and unyielding determination.

A newly formed school will have to face many challenges, just like a piece of iron to be rolled into a steel. It must undergo a thorough polish.

On this point I am proud to say:

"Having cultivated for more than 23 years without a day's break , I write on a daily basis and have 104 books to my credit. I considered this common as well as unique."

It is unique because my fate is so different from others. On one hand, I am extolled to the sky. On the other hand, I am caught in the whirlpool because of jealousy on my success. I become the most controversial character on earth.

I am well respected, I am defamed by many others at the same time.

On arrival at the Singapore International Airport, if the scene is as usual,

A thousand came to welcome me.

A hundred came to garland me.
Everybody bowed to me.
Everybody sang.

Then I would not have written this:
Master Lu Sheng-Yen is the one and only.
He is a human being full of life and blood.
He has his views and feelings.
He can sing and dance.
He has a special skill- mystic power.

Someone in the crowd saw his head was supporting a moon disc. And three Sanskrit words, Om , Ah , Hum resided in it. He quickly took his camera and took a snap. When the film was developed, Living Buddha Lian Sheng's head was really supporting a moon disc. The three Sanskrit words were very vivid.

When the photographs were circulated,
there were joys;
there was admiration;
there was nostalgia.

At the airport, one disciple said, "Grand master, please stand a little longer, let me see you more carefully, I want to have a deeper impression of you." Another disciple said, " Grand master, please slow down your pace, so that we can enjoy your charm." Yet another disciple said, "Grand master, kindly let me touch you, I shall cherish this memory." One disciple even said, " I am willing to die for Grand master, if he let me shake his hand."

Like facing others, I meet my disciples calmly. I would not grimace. Nor would I assume great airs. I am not pretentious. I am always accommodating with smiling face.

I show loving kindness to my disciples, and I have great confidence in them.

Everybody likes to see the appearance of Bodhisattva.

Wanting everybody to like me in the first instance --- even those wicked ones shall show a momentary purity, I know the reason why my head was supporting the Moon disc with Sanskrit characters.

I firmly believe:
The head of human has Moon disc,
The head of human has stars
The head of human has rays of brightness.

I am inconceivable. The Buddha is incomprehensible. And all human beings are unbelievable. Am I not lighting a lamp for all other sentient beings!

Walking on a glass bridge

In Singapore, I stayed at the Stanford hotel in the Raffles City.

Designed by the famed I.M. Pei, the hotel is an ultra modern building; one of the tallest in Singapore.

The hotel houses many restaurants, departmental stores, conference halls, and recreation centre etc.

There is one unique glass bridge. As Christmas is around the corner, the famous glass bridge is decorated with lightings and lined with all kinds of potted plants. Bright-coloured flowers and leaves lighten up the bridge.

A bridge made of glass ?

It is refreshing.

It was the first time I walked across a glass bridge. The glass is transparent, tinged with light green colour. The glass must have been hardened, as it seems unbreakable. Like glass tile, it raises from nowhere. On hearing the news, everybody just went to see it first hand.

The glass bridge can be considered a form of gracious arts. Do you agree that any form of gracious arts will attract many a follower ?

Using Master Lu Sheng-Yen's reputation as an example, many people believe that he understands the gracious arts very well; and he is able to show its special features.

Master Lu said : " Tantra uses air to build a bridge; and Tantrica uses it to transcend to the heaven."

It is astonishing that a bridge can be built out of pure air. Let me explain the hows and the whys.

"Tantra advocates the cultivation of air (i.e. Qi); and the cultivators are known as 'Qi practitioners'. Simply by eating the air initially, the accomplished practitioners can ride the air and transcend to the heaven."

The art of cultivating Qi is mastered by Tantrica. There are many oral traditions to be followed, which are highly valued by the outsiders.

Master Lu believes that there is a logical explanation to how practitioner can transcend on air-bridge. To those who choose to slander him, his view is unique, one and only.

Just like Sakyamuni Buddha, there would not be a second Master Lu Sheng-Yen in the religious fraternity. Sakyamuni Buddha is the one and only, so is Master Lu. There will not be a second one, that is why Sakyamuni Buddha said;" I am the only honoured one in the heaven and earth."

Those cultivating the air bridge will understand that:

The air is free of charge.

It is endless in supply.

It is formless and the most invincible material.

Eventually, the air will return to the void, and the ashes to the earth. If a person has more air than flesh, he will ascend; on the other hand, if he has more flesh than air, then he will surely descend.

After understanding this truth, those cultivating the air bridge will not be the same as ordinary folks. They will not have any more love, pain, slander and worries. They will know that there is nothing that cannot be solved in this world. In fact, the world has nothing to solve at all.

At the end of our life, we have to face two things: The first is "Qi"; and the second is "dust".

We always say that life is so complicated. As human nature is so different, some of us are kind, and others are bad. Many of us are not so smart; many are muddled; still others are confused and always fall into other people's plot.

As Master Lu is a practitioner of Qi, he does not believe in taking precaution against others. As a result, he always falls prey to others' tricks. But he is

8

able to laugh it off. Simply put, Master Lu Sheng-Yen is "Qi"; and those who tricked him are "dust".

Having nothing to do, I like to go strolling. The glass bridge at the Raffles City is a special one. Its glass is as smooth as a mirror. People tend to be more careful walking on a long and narrow bridge.

Just by walking across the bridge once, I was able to write an article. I do not know how many people can really understand the purpose of my article. But I am sure if they are close to my heart and have telepathy with me, they will comprehend me.

The glass bridge is unique; it is a form of gracious art. The air bridge is even more magnificent. It is the practitioner's beacon.

I consider air as the only material that is pristine (vegetarian).

Using Deva-eyes to
observe "Karma"

A two-day consultation session was arranged by the ritual organiser Yuan Xue chapter on 16th and 17th of December 1992.

What is "consultation"?

"It is solving all kinds of problems and curing strange diseases for the sentient beings!"

As we know, there is no such thing as a perfect life. Life is always full of endless problems.

I suppose Buddhas and Bodhisattvas must come to this world helping mankind to solve their problems.

What will make Master Lu Sheng-Yen a happy man ? To tell the truth, he will be very happy when he is able to solve other people's problem.

Fronting the audience, I see among the crowds, all kinds of friends,

— some suffering from terminal illness,
— a newly-born that is deformed,
— a divorced woman with sorrowful look,
— a ruthless drunken man
— some unenlightened practitioners
— a dumb, deaf, and handicapped beggar.

A half-paralysed man came to me, he berated, "I am upright, and do nothing wrong in my whole life. I am unassuming, why must I be suffering from such sickness? You tell me whether there is any justice? There is no law of Karma, since kind people have to suffer, and the wicked ones were off the hooks. There are no heavenly principles in this world any longer. Please enlighten me !"

Using my deva-eyes, I saw him pointing to the sky, and made a curse, then he broke the neck of Amitabha Buddha's image; and threw the image of Avalokitesvara Bodhisattva into his toilet.

I related this incident. His daughter was nodding her head. "My father is OK. The only problem with him is he likes to take up the cudgels for the injured party. Although he has done a lot of good deeds, he makes silly mistakes too. He was angry with me when I prayed to Buddha and Avalokitesvara Bodhisattva. How can he get angry with the divine ?"

Her father is a wonderful person who likes to go against the divinity. Agitated, he suffered from a stroke, and became paralysed.

A middle-aged lady with lots of "negative forces" in her face also came to see me. Using deva-eyes, I saw many mahjong tables in her house. People were gambling there. Many card-ghosts converged at her house. The woman contracted negative forces as a result.

I asked her, "Do you gamble ?" She replied, "I do not know how to gamble, and I don't gamble." I asked again,"If you do not know how to gamble, why is it that you have so many gambling tables at home ? " She answered, "Lian Sheng, you are really a living Buddha. My house is full of gambling tables, and my son-in-law is running the gambling den. I am just helping out there by doing some chores."

I advised her to close the gambling den. Or simply move out from that place. Her negative forces will disappear at once.

A female disciple came to consult me about her shrine at home. Using deva-eyes to see, I said, "In the centre is Cundi, mother of all Buddhas, what a good choice. Franked by protectors Skanda on the left and Jia Nan on the right. The photograph of PadmaKumara is quite spiritual. I smell the scent of flower, the fragrance of tulips." She screamed, "Grand master, you have a very sharp sense. This morning I just offered a few stalks of tulip."

Her scream drew quite a few people's attention. They were amazed at the accuracy of what I have seen.

This is Master Lu Sheng-Yen. My colourful life

is full of mysterious experience. It is legendary.

Maybe because of this, wherever Master Lu went, miracles happened and strange things occurred.

His experience and story are both magnificent and unpredictable. His life is full of stimulus, too numerous to write.

A story of a woman
who cannot conceive

I come across many incidence that are both funny and annoying during consultation sessions. Human beings are so inconceivable, they have fascinating behaviour.

I find them interesting. And they find me even more amazing.

A bright and lovable, longhaired girl told me during consultation. "Grand master, your prediction is totally out !"

"Why ?" I was dumbfounded.

"I still do not have a child, " She said.

"Did you ask me to help before ?" I could not recall.

"I wrote to you in Seattle, and even took six courses of heavenly-bestowed pregnancy talisman, and I do not conceive."

"Is that so ?" I blushed.

I had quite a lot of excitements in my life. Most of those who asked favour from me would find gradual changes in their lives. Their business will be getting better. Those without child will become parent, matrimonial relationship will improve, strange sickness will be cured, and fame and status ensue...

During the consultation session, I help others to clear their doubts and cure their strange sickness. If there is no improvement, it would be a waste of time.

I told her, "I don't believe the six courses of heavenly-bestowed pregnancy talisman can be so ineffective. I will write one more talisman for you, I am sure this time it will work."

"Why must the talisman work today ?" she asked.

"Because new one signifies change," I answered.

When I was writing the talisman, suddenly no magic power passed through my hand and my pen. This has not happened under normal circumstances. The talisman must have magic power, otherwise, it is useless. I knew for sure the talisman I wrote will be ineffective.

I looked up and asked her,

"Miss, could you please explain further, why after taking the talisman you are still not expecting ?" I asked the same old question.

Adamantly, the girl replied, "All the problems are more or less the same in this world, only they come in different forms. Since you asked me again, I shall tell you frankly. I had my womb removed long ago, due to infection."

"Why don't you say so", suddenly I am enlightened.

"How do I know ?" the girl replied.

"Master Lu has mystic power, and the talisman is known as heavenly-bestowed pregnancy charm, I thought I will have a child. It does not matter whether I have a womb or not". "I.....", I was speechless.

Master Lu is a Vajra Living Buddha who has all kinds of mystic powers. To her, everything should be possible. But sad to say, sometimes it is impossible.

The sentiments of being baffled and finding no way out makes me feel lonely, dispirited and frustrated. I have a deep feeling of remorse. There are many imperfections and inequity in this world. But I am all alone, what else can I do ? Like this young woman who could not conceive a baby, She must be given a new womb, then she can be made pregnant.

Most people do believe that master Lu is a Living Buddha, a dharma king. He is adored and admired because of his high status. The rich and famous would like to get to know him. He stays in the presidential suite, and drives a Rolls Royce. And

16

yet his benevolence remains unchanged.

His feeling is not well understood, worse still sometimes misunderstood by many. In fact, he lives in deep sorrow, may be as a result of his fame.

He is famous because he has many friends and disciples. He is infamous because he has many foes and enemies.

There is one way he must walk, as a last resort, he must live in seclusion, without itinerary, and disappearing without a trace !

Headline in the Lian-Ho Evening News

Mr. Chen Zhen, the chief editor of Lian-Ho Evening News in Singapore sent a senior reporter, Mr Ou Fu Li, to Raffles City Hotel on 17 December 1992 to interview me.

A week later on 24th December, the following headline appeared in the news:

"A controversial character in the religious field, Living Buddha Lu Sheng-Yen came to Singapore on a propagation tour."

"Candidates of the US presidential election consulted him."

"He is said to have possessed certain mystic powers."

"According to Master Lu, heresy is when a religion walks on the wrong path."

Occupied quite a big column, the news continued for three days.

On seeing the publicity, the True Buddha disciples were very happy. Master Lu Sheng-Yen and True Buddha school suddenly became a hot topic in the local news.

Other schools were adamant and claimed that the offensive publicity was coordinated to culminate in the final ritual. The thought itself is ridiculous. It is absurd. Lian Hua Li Na, a disciple of mine, is a family friend of the chief editor.

The chief editor once asked her. "In what way can I help you ?" Lian Hua Li Na said :"My teacher, Living Buddha Lian Sheng is coming from the States of America soon. He is a Living Buddha who advocates practical cultivation. I wish you could learn something from him."

As a result of this, Lian Ho Evening News reported the event in three consecutive days.

We did not plan any publicity, let alone finale. The commotion created by the news media was triggered off by the statement made by Lian Hua Li Na.

It has been said :"Lu Sheng-Yen is an active volcano. He has been restrained by the traditional schools for a long while. Ousted, attacked and hunted by them , he has been the victim of rumour for umpteen years. One of these days, the volcano will erupt and the lava soars all over."

The world will change its colour,

The universe will have a deluge.

The history of religion will have a new page.

It is also said,"Lu Sheng-Yen outwardly shows he is cool and expressionless. In fact, he is an active volcano."

On these views, may I say that, "I am an ordinary person. I am not a piece of wood , nor a rock. I am not a piece of ice, nor am I a legendary volcano. I am not lunatic, although sometimes I behave like one."

For the sake of walking the path to the truth, I am capable of doing what others can't do. I have made a vow to sacrifice my life for the succour of all sentient beings. I am willing to burn myself like a torch, so as to bring brightness to others.

Knowing all the truth , all the dharma in this universe, I am the one and only person to have achieved this level, that is why I dare to say my enlightenment is magnificent. I am more than willing to impart my wisdom to all the sentient beings.

I am the messenger of Buddha. I come with a mission to succour lives, to help other people gain enlightenment. I am definitely not a butcher.

I am just an ordinary folk, who lives in this samsara world. Harbouring no ill-will, I do not have a master plan. I will die a natural death like anybody else. Remember, even the most intelligent person who possesses the most magnificent tantra will have to go through the stages of "form, existence, deform and decay".

Lian Ho Evening News also touched on the rarity of having sarira in the remains. People from religious fraternity know that only one person can cause the dead convicts to have sarira in their remains, and he is none other than Master Lu Sheng-Yen.

The incidence is not only bizarre and mysterious. It is a sacred event. It is the best evidence to prove the adage "laying down the butcher's knife and one can be an instant Buddha."

Some may conclude that, "May be this is the reason why Master Lu Sheng-Yen is considered "a new star is born" in the religious world."

Four columns were used by Singapore's Lian Ho Evening News to report on Living Buddha Lian Sheng's propagational tour in Singapore on 24th December 1992.

The headline was :"The controversial character in the religious field, Living Buddha Lian Sheng, arrived in Singapore for propagation." The reports almost occupied the whole page. Among others, the reporter said "I have tried. By giving him a few names, he was able to give me an account of their whereabouts and problems facing them."

Other points discussed during the interviews are extracted as follows:

Reporter: "How do we distinguish between religion and politics?"

Living Buddha: "Religion is purely a cultivation of mind. It should not be linked to politics. Politics concerns the management of people, while religion manages the minds of the people. Since time immemorial, religion is used to interfere with politics. It is no easy task to separate the two of them. To learn Buddhism, we must use our wisdom and intelligence objectively. Cultivate ourselves with open mind. The religious world will have no quarrel if we just do that."

Reporter: "Is it true that employees of the last few Presidential nominees in the States of America came to consult you ?"

Living Buddha: "Before the US presidential elections, employees of the nominees came to consult me. Whether they were under instruction or acted out of curiosity, that I could not tell."

Reporter: "Master Lu is also known as Living Buddha. What is the difference between a living Buddha and Dalai Lama ?"

Living Buddha: "In terms of status all Living Buddha

are equal. It is not necessary to find out whose status is higher. If we can cultivate to the extent of capable of controlling our life and death, and the Buddha nature appears, we are Living Buddha. The appearance of Buddha nature is more important than the status."

Reporter: "Lately there have been many cults appearing in different parts of the world. How do they have the powers to control their followers ?"

Living Buddha:"Heresy is a religious belief that moves along the wrong path; and go against what is considered as a good tradition. It is seeking the truth from external, unlike all the righteous religions that advocate cultivate internally. Every religion will have its power, and this cannot be denied. The question is how do we go about inducing these powers. In short, power derives from concentration. The cults that flourish these few years harbour ill-will. They are used to achieve personal gain and for illegal purposes.

All major forms of religion including catholicism, christianity and others embody the Buddhist dharma. The only difference lies in the level of attainment. All religions are good."

When reporting the news , the reporters were impressed by the broad-mindedness and temperament of Living Buddha Lian Sheng. Skimming over such topics as "mystic powers" casually, Living Buddha Lian Sheng who is a soft speaker, was able to convince them that he never indulges in loud and empty talk.

The experience of taking a trishaw ride

We took trishaw from Raffles City to Clifford pier at about 9 a.m. on 18 December 1992.

Singapore's trishaw has its carriage and an extra wheel on the left hand side of the bicycle proper.

I had taken trishaw ride in Taiwan when I was young. The trishaw in Taiwan is different from that of Singapore. In Taiwan, the puller sits in front and the passengers behind. The seat is very spacious. With a moveable curtain, the trishaw can be operational rain and shine. The trishaw puller in Singapore sits on the right, and the passengers on the left. The seat is comparatively small; the carriage is just like a baby pram attaching to a bicycle.

What do you think of the trishaw ? It is something new, and quite satisfying , I answered.

A gloomy day it was! The tropical heat was swept aside by the drizzling rain. The wind blew towards us, once the trishaw moved,it was quite comfortable.

The land in Singapore is quite flat, there are many man-made gardens. The ever present greenery together with numerous flowers made the humid island a lively and bright place to live in. Towards the sea, the scenery is even more beautiful. The sound of waves bring life to the modern city. The beautiful sight is full of vibration and energy.

I came to appreciate how relax it is to go sightseeing with a trishaw. We passed through many modern buildings, city hall, the sea nearby is as clear as a mirror. Flowers and trees were everywhere, and we came across the famous Merlion statue.

Groups and groups of tourists went by. The citizens are law- abiding; and the surroundings spotlessly clean. In such an environment, we forget about our troubles and our minds are very calm.

The trishaw puller entertained us by making a few extra rounds at the pedestrian walkway. The speeding vehicles zoomed pass us from the main road on our right. On our left was a big piece of grass-land which borders the endless sea.

It gave us the heroic spirit when we rode through vehicles and high-rise building. I appreciate the lofty sentiments in taking the trishaw ride.

I always believe that Singapore's way of life must be very colourful. It is just a natural phenomena for an ultra modern city like Singapore to offer such a wide variety of choice in life.

But it has the gracious facet as well. For instance,

the people living here, the friendship and the code of brotherhood of the disciples. Their hearts are so warm , just like the summer sun that could melt the ice from the northern hemisphere.

Guru Lian Xiang said she liked Singapore. I said Singapore is a fine country.
The trishaw puller started to chat with me.

"Can you speak Mandarin, Master ?"

"Yes, I can."

"Master, your look gives me the impression that you do quite a lot of personal cultivation."

I smiled, telling my self that the trishaw puller knows how to tell fortune also.

Casually, I remarked ,"You look quite an upright person !"

"Master, it is alright to be upright. But I am always the object of bully, and taken for a ride. Those who claimed to be my friends sweet-talked me, and betrayed me. They are so ungrateful and tried to chop me into pieces."

He did not stop complaining for quite a while.

"Those who said that they would not harm me are the ones that did so."

"Those who said they wanted to return a favour to me were the ones that wanted me dead."

"Friends are supposed to be on the same side,

but they were as sinister as a snake."

"What am I supposed to do with this kind of people ?"

I was speechless.

As a controversial person, it is not uncommon for me to cause contentions. Whether I am alive or otherwise, there are many topics for them to dispute.

I came across an interesting event. A difficult, rude and unreasonable disciple of mine once told me , "I will never cause harm to you, Grand master. It is not my style. I want to repay your favour with all my heart and soul."

And now, she is distributing all kinds of booklets slandering me – Master Lu Sheng-Yen.

On hearing what the trishaw puller had just said, I am really dumbfounded. (like a dumb person tasting bitter herbs)

Kusu island

We arrived at Kusu island, one of the smallest island at the southern part of Singapore at noon of December 18,1992.

There are two temples on the island. One is for the local god; another for the Datok (A malay title). The latter is built on the slope of the only knoll in the island. These two temples are not far apart.

Why is the island known as Kusu (Turtle island)? May be the shape of the island looks like a turtle. The reputations of these two temples are well known in the vicinity. The annual pilgrimage is well attended by the believers. The sight is spectacular when sticks of incense are burnt.

Kusu island is really small; almost as small as a ship. Apart from a small garden , it is surrounded by endless water. The sea water sparkles under the golden light just like a folded skirt of a passionate young lady. The dense smell of the sea follows the transparent breeze, it is refreshing. I took a few deep breaths, enjoying the breeze to my heart's content.

My impression is that the sea water is extraordinary blue. And the blue is so pure and penetrating. A feeling of mighty current ripples in the bottom of my heart.

Surrounded by many small islands, Singapore could be considered an island country-- albeit when compared with Philippines and Indonesia, a country with more than a thousand islands, the surrounding islands of Singapore are just too small.

We went to tour the local god temple first. It could be considered the show piece of the island although it is very small. The local god is enshrined in the center. (Local god is also the fortune god.) The side halls house Avaloketisvara Bodhisattva and the eight immortals of the Taoist faith.

I do not know the history of this small temple. It does not have any grandeur to show. There are ponds around the temple, when it is high tide, sea water will fill the ponds, which a few concrete turtles are placed.

Cupping my hands, I paid my respects. In my deep concentration, I saw the true-self of the local god. (What the local god was in his previous life.) He pleaded with me not to divulge his secret. I did not utter a word.

Then we went to visit and pay respect to the Datok. Built on a big piece of rock on the steep slope, and surrounded by trees, the temple does not look like one. The access is a narrow path. It is more a family shrine. Altar tables are erected for the Datok, his wife, his son and his daughter. There are no images, only a few pieces of rock behind the altars. Cupping my hands , I paid my respects.

Someone asked me, "Why do you pray to local god and Datok here ?"

I replied, "There was a causation. The last time I had a ritual at the Toa Payoh Indoor Stadium, many gods attended the function. Two of them whom I did not know, told me they were from Kusu Island. One spoke in Mandarin, and the other in Malay. They invited me to Kusu Island. That is how I come to know the place and tour the island today."

Someone asked again, "Master Lu Sheng-Yen, did local god and Datok come to welcome you just now ?"

I smiled and did not answer.

Both the local god and Datok asked me not to reveal a word about them, that is why I just smiled. Normally based on my character, I would tell people what I know, since there is no secret in this world.

But the two gods pleaded with me not to reveal their secrets, lest they should have troubles and rumours to deal, I agreed to keep quiet and not to say a word.

They wanted some privacy. Their representations are protected by the law of karma. I will have to face the consequences if I leak them.

That is why I had to say, "I could not tell."

The correct knowledge and correct view of Li Mu Yuan.

The executive in charge of Singapore Buddhist Lodge, Mr Li Mu Yuan, a Kulapaty (laity) came to visit Grand master at the hotel he stayed on December 18th, 1992, during Grand master's propagation tour to Singapore.

(Below is an excerpt of conversation between Grand master (**G**) and Li Mu Yuan (**L**))

G. Thank you for coming. You have given such a great help to the dead convicts.

L. This is my duty. But there are many Singaporeans who misunderstood these kind-hearted dead convicts. In fact, I will help them no matter which school of Buddhism they belonged to. I want to cooperate with others.

Those dead convicts put in a lot of effect in their cultivation. For instance, after the cremation of Lian Hua Bao Cheng, we found two pieces of colourful sarira in his remains. His sisters sent them from the prison to the Singapore Buddhist Lodge, a journey of 30 minutes' drive, another piece of sarira had grown already. It is inconceivable!

We tried to break them with a hammer, but to no avail. Another True Buddha disciple who used to have good cultivation. But at the last moment, he lost his temper and started to scold others. All his virtue was wiped off, his face bled, and there was no sarira.

It is very difficult to cultivate in the prison. But they encouraged one another, studied and did chanting together. Without any guidance, it was very difficult. It reaffirms the Buddhist saying :"Putting down the butcher's knife, and become an instant Buddha."

G. These people converged here with a cause. They had cultivated for many lives. Since they had made mistakes this life, they wanted to set good examples for other buddhists, and encouraged them to do cultivation. To them, this is their only hope.

L. Some Taiwanese came to ask me whether those sarira are genuine. Since I can't tell lie , I told them the truth.

G. Dharma masters and other follow cultivators who heard the news were sceptical. They wrote to seek confirmation. Some of them even joined hand to protest against me. In fact the sarira is an encouragement for the dead convicts, their only hope. People should not oppose the sarira of dead convicts because just because they do not like True Buddha School.

L. Some convicts cultivated the prostration continuously until black marks left between their eyebrows!

M. I am moved by this.

L. They cultivated personally, and their results are seen by others. As a result, their family members also took refuge and are full of confidence now.

M. Thank you very much.

L. Don't mention it. It is very difficult to succour these dead convicts. There are very few monks who are visiting the prison. Moreover, your books are very difficult to come by, they had to take turn to read the books. The seed you sowed is bearing fruits now. A dead convict took refuge two months before his execution. He was a scoundrel before. He used faeces to throw at others , rubbed at others, and destroyed the images of gods. When he took refuge even his family members could not believe it.

G. He was succoured by Buddha and Bodhisattva.

Not me.

L. Why don't you clarify in public ?

G. It is difficult, people are very stubborn. They scolded me wherever I go, and even printed a lot of booklets to slander me. I have spoken enough. We are a new school. The slanders will continue unabated. When I was young, I rebutted whenever I was defamed. And now, I let nature take its course. But even then, the slanders did not reduce. This is what happened for the last few years.

L. You come to preside over a ritual?

M. I have given three sermons already. The final one will be a ritual. Our ritual is empowered by Buddha and Bodhisattva, and protected by Vajra protectors. We believe in results. Some dharma masters and monks may show Mudra, recite sutras on the stage but there were no spiritual response by the participants. But our rituals are different. After the souls deliverance ritual, the participant's deceased relatives would tell him that they were uplifted and they had benefited from the well- conducted ritual. The results can be used to help the spread of Buddhism.

Life is so short, there is nothing to fight for, as

long as we try our best to do until we are dead, there will be no regrets. Like the dead convicts, we are walking on a road of no return. So is the cultivating path. No matter how big the defamation is, I shall try my best without regrets.

L. We can't recede on our cultivation.

M. There are many people who vowed not to recede, but soon they gave up. That is why Buddha once said as long as you can keep your first vow, you are sure to be enlightened as a Buddha. The first vow is of utmost importance.

L. Bother you for so long, I shall take my leave now.

M. Thank you for coming. I am glad to have met all of you.

L. I should thank you instead. As long as it is correct, we must do it. We don't care about the rest.

This is the first time Living Buddha met Mr. Li Mu Yuan. Mr. Li has been with the Singapore Buddhist Lodge for more than two decades. Although he is not a True Buddha disciple, he has the correct knowledge and correct view.

Before he left, he presented a wooden image of Sakyamuni Buddha to Grand Master. In return,

Grand master gave him a rosary beads made of Bodhi seeds. The dharma bliss filled the meeting place.

This is the first time I met Mr. Li Mu Yuan. He is not a True Buddha disciple of me. He gave me the impression that he is a honest and sincere cultivator, who has regular features and is capable of upholding justice.

The news that dead convicts had sarira in their remains travel wide and fast; and the person who discovered the sarira is non other than Li Mu Yuan.

Those who disagree with me said, "Impossible! ", "Fabrication!" and "A lie!"

I want to tell you one thing, Li Mu Yuan belongs to Singapore Buddhist Lodge, he does not have any connection with True Buddha School, why must he lie or fabricate for us ? Other things which are well recognised:

The sarira is genuine; Li Mu Yuan is a real kulapaty .

To tell the truth, there is only one person that could shock the whole world (past, present, local and overseas), and he is non other than Living Buddha Lian Sheng, Master Lu Sheng-Yen.

Have you ever heard of the news that a dead convict had sarira before?

It is nothing strange for a venerated monk to have sarira.

It is a great news alright, for a dead convict to have sarira.

It is fated in Lu Sheng-Yen's life that a lot of inconceivable things will happen to him. Many of his disciples are unusual people too, and they will have unusual stories to tell.

Stories related to Lu Sheng-Yen are always stimulating and full of excitements.

Dead convict-scoundrel Sarira-A fruit for people who gained enlightenment

Linking these two together, the story will interest and shock many people. Nevertheless, it is true. The fact that dead convicts had sarira in their remains reminds us that master Lu Sheng-Yen can use his mystic power to fly and hide in the ground, to change himself into many forms.

Lian hua jia xing told his personal experience – A special interview by Guru Cheng Ren

In order that the Buddhism fraternity all over the world can understand why the dead convicts can have sarira in their remains, the writer interviewed Lian Hua Jia Xing , a True Buddha disciple who was once sentenced to death in Singapore.

(In its 17th edition, the True Buddha News made Lian Hua Bing Fa the headline after he was acquitted from the death sentence)

Question : Lian Hua Jia Xing, why were you sentenced to death in the first place ?

Answer   : Because of drug trafficking.

Question : How old are you now ?

Answer   : I am thirty four.

Question : When did you commit the crime ?

Answer   : In 1985 (i.e. Seven years ago.)

Question : Do you know the rest of True Buddha disciples then awaiting their execution ?

Answer   : I know all of them. In fact, Lian Hua Yu

Xing came to prison the same time as me. We are one of the earliest to have taken refuge.

Question : How do you take refuge ? And when did you start the cultivation?

Answer : At first, I practised Nichiren Shoshu Buddhism, and chanted Namo Horen Gekyo for nine hours daily. While Lian Hua Yu Xing chanted the great compassion mantra and recited the name of Avalokitesvara Bodhisattva. But we did not experience any spiritual response even after one year. One day in 1987, Lian Hua Yu Xing's wife brought him a few books written by the Grand master. We started reading them and found what were expounded in the books to be true. We were so moved by the contents that we started to cry.

I learned from Lian Hua Yu Xing the way to recite the name of Avalokitesvara. After three days of recital, when I faced the wall, I felt the pain that was beyond description, I came to realise that life is nothing but sorrow and impermanence. While reciting the name of Avalokitesvara, I pleaded with him to save my life. Suddenly, everything around me faded away, and Avalokitesvara Bodhisattva stood in front of me. Dressed in white and taller than a few storey, he radiated golden lights. Two lads, his attendants were standing beside him.

He asked whether I knew him. I replied that I knew him as I dreamed about him five months ago, and I missed him very much. To my question of whether I could take refuge in Master Lu Sheng-Yen who lives in Seattle, he answered affirmatively. Suddenly the Grandmaster appeared vividly from the ground and floated in the air, then he faded away gradually. Avalokitesvara assured me that as long as I cultivated the tantra, I would be released after serving five years in the prison for what I had committed. After the departure of the Bodhisattva, there were trace of fragrance in the room. I told Lian Hua Yu Xing the miracle I saw, and both of us took refuge together immediately.

Question : What are the living conditions in the

prison ?

Answer   : Since all of us were sentenced to death, we had our own rooms, which was enough for a bed and a toilet bowl. Apart from eating and bathing, we had to be in our cells. Before taking refuge in True Buddha Tantra, it was unbearable. All the convicts indulged in singing, talking loudly and scolding one another. All of us were quarrelsome.

Question : Any change after taking refuge ?

Answer   : The situation did not improve when we started the cultivation. Those who took refuge were very quiet and cultivated the tantra whole-heartedly. We learned the four foundations from "Top secrets of True Buddha School" without any teacher. As we had not seen a picture of Vajrasattva before, so we had to base on what was written in the book to do the visualisation. The spiritual response came slightly more than a month later. Whenever we visualised the image of Vajrasattva, Grandmaster's face would appear. All of us agreed to use Grand master's face when we visualised Vajrasattva. We were glad to have done that.

With full confidence, all of us were serious about our cultivation. The prison was turned into a retreat centre. Apart from eating and bathing, all of us remained in our cells all the time. There was hardly any noise since no one talked, or singed any more. The cells were just like isolated ones. We just carried on our chanting and did a few rounds of cultivations daily. Doing great prostration to atone for misbehaviour, we hit our heads against the floor so hard that our foreheads were blackened and smooth.

It could say we turned the prison into a pure land. With unceasing effort, everybody knows the destination clearly. Then we took a step further, we started to cultivate Padmakumara dharma, so as to embody ourselves with Padmakumara. We had dharma bliss as all of us had spiritual responses.

Question : What is the cause of your release from the prison ?

Answer   : The powers of Grand master, Buddha and Bodhisattva. In fact, my release or otherwise is immaterial. Only a true accomplished cultivator can be considered to have achieved freedom in life. I missed all of them very much and would cherish the time we spent together in the prison.

All of us could verify what Grand master said during the ritual held on 19th, "Grand master always came to the prison to empower us !"

Once suffering from gastralgia , I prayed for the empowerment by Grandmaster. Immediately, I felt a hand empowering my head. My head became numb, and feverish. And the pain of my stomach subsided. Everything was alright thereafter.

Question : How do you feel about the news that the dead convicts had sarira in their remains ?

Answer : I knew Lian Hua Yu Xing was emotionally stable the night before his execution. He slept well and had full confidence in Grand master, Buddha and Bodhisattva. He was still chanting the guru's mantra when the execution was carried out. He even smiled to say goodbye to us. Like what he wrote: "Without Grand master's guidance, I dare say, no one will be able to pass the life so elegantly."

Question : Do you have anything to add ?

Answer   : I have just told you the truth. The True
Buddha Tantra as expounded by the
Grand master is very magnificent. I am
willing to be a witness to confirm the
truth.

Both ex-dead convicts Lian Hua Bing Fa and
Lian Hua Jia Xing have personally testified that
sarira were found in the remains of the convicts
executed.

They are both tall and thin; they have to be so.
As the news of sarira caused a furore, they are often
asked by the buddhists all over the world whether
that is true.

In our society, dead convicts are full of stigma;
let alone qualify to gain enlightenment. They are
doomed to be plunged into the hell. Their future
fates are condemned by ordinary people.

They are also human. If they really repent for
what they have done, they can be as pure as can be.
They too can be saints after cultivation. Using
unceasing effort in pursuing Buddhism, they can gain
enlightenment also. Their souls can be ascended to
the Western Pure Land.

I will spare no effort in saving my disciples, amongst them are the greatest dead convicts, prostitutes, drunkards, and assassins.

It is not unnatural that some of my disciples wanted me dead. This is no laughing matter. They are the greatest rebels.

As human is mortal, there is no exception for the dead convicts and me. I would rather die in the hands of my own disciples than outsiders.

Someone said : "Master Lu Sheng-Yen will surely die one of these days. But his spirit will always remain in the hearts of millions. "

What they said are true. When the news of dead convicts have sarira. in their remains spread, master Lu Sheng-Yen just took it with a smile. When his rebellious disciples sold him out, his lofty sentiments did not recede. Although his laughter could break the roof tiles, he still managed to sing the chorus. He did not even get himself drunk.

I smiled when the dead convicts had sarira. I also smiled when the rebellious disciples betrayed me.

My smile is bright and clean; and full of mystery.

The following is a fact. For the last few years , the True Buddha school has been the focus of world religions. The name of Master Lu Sheng-Yen appeared almost daily as the headline in politics, social and cultural pages of the newspapers. All kinds of magazines that have a wide readership use master Lu's picture as over page instead of some actresses. There is nobody more controversial than master Lu yet.

In Hong Kong, someone on the street pointed at me and said, "Look, this is the Living Buddha appearing in the front page." In Malaysia, the chef came out of the kitchen and exclaimed, " Look, this is the Living Buddha that is the man of the hour."

They used such terms as "Flower light carefree Buddha", "Maya", "Sari Buddha", "Heresy", "Righteous Buddhism", "pagan", "trickster","woman killer", "a gentleman", etc to describe me. But there is no consensus.

I just laugh it off when they came to ask me. There is no conclusion when I am alive, nor will they be any change after my death. The line between a genius and a madman is a very thin one. To those who like me, I am talented. For others, I am just a lunatic.

Forget about what they have just said, and listen to the truth I am telling you now:

Many dead convicts all over the world have taken refuge in Living Buddha Lian Sheng and they are cultivating True Buddha Tantra now. I am not sure whether the dead convicts made True Buddha Tantra well known or the other way round.

Which is the cause, and which is the effect ? There is no creator in this instance. The sarira found in the remains of the dead convicts were not created. They were formed naturally.

The sarira is to reaffirm what Sakyamuni Buddha said previously : "All human beings have Buddha nature in them. Putting down the Butcher's knife and be enlightened as an instant Buddha."

In short, the dead convicts were merely confirming what the Buddha said.

Killing and Committing arson

Time: 2 p.m.
Date: December 19, 1992
Place: Singapore IMM building
Crowds: Around 20,000 attending the Tantric ritual organised by Yuan Xue Chapter, and assisted by Yuan Zhen and Yuan Xi chapters.

A huge picture of Padmakumara served as the backdrop. While the ritual was in progress....

A suspicious looking man slipped into the backstage when no one was watching him. Taking out a few pieces of papers, he dipped them into petrol. He tried to start a fire with the lighter, by burning the picture of Padmakumara. I was sitting in front of the picture.

Although the papers dipped with petrol were ablaze, nothing happened. To prevent this sort of sabotage from happening, more than 50 policemen and plain-clothed security personnel were posted outside the building long before the commencement of the ritual. Moreover more than 50 of our own security personnel were also deployed inside the building. An additional 20 people were patrolling the ritual site. That is why when the fire flashed, it was immediately spotted by the patrol team.

The culprit, on seeing three of the guards rushing to him, shouted: "We are the righteous Buddhism!". Then he sped away, merging with the crowd and disappeared immediately. At first the patrol leader wanted to make an announcement on the fire, then he decided otherwise since the fire was already put out by his team. Stepping up the patrol inside the building, he awaited the end of the ritual.

As the ritual was carried out smoothly, I heard the incidence and footsteps, even the spraying sound of extinguisher. The whole commotion was over in a short while.

If the fire really broke out and we announced the bad news, the death toll would be very high, as the whole building was full of people, even the corridors and car parks were fully occupied. The lifts and exits of IMM building would not be adequate in this instance. Imagine 20,000 people all rushing out at once, stepping on one another. I am sure a lot of people will be hurt. (In Hong Kong the mishaps at Lan Gui Fan, 22 people died and many more injured because of the rushing crowds.)

The incidence can be considered an attempted murder and attempted arson.

What is the motive of doing this ?

They consider themselves the righteous, and we are the opposite.

Like a typhoon passing through the world, True Buddha School affects those who claimed to be the righteous schools of Buddhism quite a lot.

They torn our publicity posters.

They blackened out the time and venue of our notices of rituals to be held.

They cut the banners put up by us.

They placed negative news and advertisement in the newspapers.

They even distributed booklets attacking me personally.

And the latest is attempted murder and arson. I wondered those who claimed to be from the righteous school of Buddhism could tell me of all the karma created, which is the most serious offence? I can't think of one that is even more critical than killing and committing arson.

Sometimes I joked about being evil. Tell me my wickedness and the vices of True Buddha Tantra.

Facing an avalanche of slanders and charged with instantaneous explosive, I encountered a great set-back, but I still persisted in propagating the True Buddha Tantra. I have done nothing wrong.

To think it objectively, those who claimed to be from the righteous schools of Buddhism can be very cruel, sometimes really heartless.

But we still welcome them with a smile.

Most people have the misconception that the religious world must be very peaceful, they are very wrong about this. Wars had been waged, blood shed and arms used. The True Buddha School as founded by Master Lu Sheng-Yen does not seek to destroy other schools, nor other religions. We believe in harmony and perfection and never to use force.

It is a pity that the so called righteous schools of Buddhism had to resort to using violence to deal with our school.

What shall we do now ?

I , Lu Sheng-Yen still insist that:

We must condone them.

We must be patient with them.

We must be accommodating.

We must move them with our attainments in cultivation.

The inner meanings of "Pu Men" Chapter

Time : 2.00 p.m.
Date : 19 December 1992
Venue : Singapore IMM building

Twenty thousand people attended the sermon on the inner meanings of "Pu Men" chapter, given by Living Buddha Lian Sheng.

"Pu Men " chapter mentions:

"Chanting the name of Avalokitesvara Bodhisattva, by virtue of his powers, you will not be burnt by the fire, even if you are in a sea of fire."

I am asked to explain :

"The fire mentioned here is no ordinary fire. It is the inner restless and salacious fire of human beings. Avalokitesvara can turn our senses of hearing off, and these fires would be dampened. Once the outer fire is extinguished, the inner one will be put out immediately.

"Pu Men" chapter mentions:

"The Bodhisattva uses his power of self-realisation to prevent human beings from drowning even they fall into water. "

I am asked to explain:

"The water mentioned here is no ordinary water. It is the inner water such as blood and excrement of human beings. Before we die, we tend to see the earth submerges into the water. With the mystic powers, Avalokitesvara Bodhisattva imparts us the skill of "hearing by seeing". Once we have mastered the skill, our inner water will dry up and the outer water subside. "

"Pu Men" chapter mentions:

"If the ship is blown into a demon country by evil wind, as long as one of the passengers recites the name of Avalokitesvara, all will be saved from such misfortune."

I am asked to explain:

"This is no ordinary wind. It is our inner ignorant wind, which causes waves of thoughts passing through our confused state of mind. Avalokitesvara Bodhisattva teaches us to be detached from our surroundings, and our heart will be tranquil. Without attachment, environment will be absolute. When there is calm and tranquil, the inner wind will subside and the outer wind will also calm down. This is the manifestation of mystic powers of Avalokitesvara Bodhisattva."

"Pu Men" chapter mentions:

"A person who is due to be killed, recites the name of Avalokitesvara Bodhisattva, the murder weapons (knives and sticks) will break into pieces, and he will be saved."

I am asked to explain:

"The knives and sticks mentioned here refer to our cracking bones. As Avalokitesvara Bodhisattva has mastered the Vajra samadhi and illusory samadhi, as long as we cultivate these dharma, we will be able to obtain the Vajra indestructible and illusory body. That is why when knife and stick hit the body, the weapons will break into pieces. It is like chopping the water--an illusory transformation."

We were talking about the four elements of "fire", "water", "wind", and "earth".

Most ordinary Buddhists think that "Pu Men" chapter from the Lotus Sutra is one of the most elementary text. It is easy to recite and comprehend. But I am of the view that it is easy to recite but very difficult to comprehend.

To me, the sutra is not only elegant outwardly. It is also full of inner realisation and mentality. It is one of the most profound Sutras. It is simple and yet difficult.

"Not burn in fire, not drown in water, saved from demon and destruction of weapons."

It sounds simple and yet not really so.

"Pu Men" Chapter is always considered a Sutrayana Sutra.

Outwardly it appears to be so. But strictly speaking, it is a Sutra of Tantrayana. It manifests a perfection of inner cultivation of Earth, Water, Fire, Wind and Emptiness. It is much more than just for reciting only.

To me, Avalokitesvara has four inconceivables:

  (1) His Mantra

  (2) His transformations

  (3) His omnipresent salvation

  (4) His granting of wishes to all directions

I am the person who has the full comprehension of "Pu Men" chapter. Thus, I know the interpretation of :

"The past Buddha by the name of "True and Bright", now manifests as Avalokitesvara. He has accumulated the magnificent virtue and assumed the form of thousand arms and eyes. With great compassion, he radiates lights to the dharma realms, and protects all sentient beings. He teaches them to follow the Bodhi path and recite the perfect Mantra."

True Buddha Empowerment

I was feted to Johor Bahru from Singapore's Raffles City on 20 December 1992 at 4.p.m. by a Malaysian guru Mr Yang Zhong Zhi.

It is very convenient to travel from Singapore to Malaysia. All you have to do is clear the immigration and custom of both countries.

The officers at the Singapore immigration and custom department heard the news of my arrival. They decided to take refuge in me. A ceremony was held immediately. We were then brought to tour the drug detection facilities.

The checking at the Malaysia custom was more stringent. But one of the officers recognised me and asked, "Are you Master Lu Sheng-Yen ?" "Yes, I am, How do you know me ?" I answered with a question. "I have read your books." I was able to clear the custom without opening my luggage.

I said in the car, "As a famous person, I do have privilege to get special treatment. But at times, people will be more fastidious towards me." A happy and yet painful thought surged in my minds alternately for the two extreme ways of treatment. Too good a treatment is not good, so is too thorough a check. There are just too many things in this world, I am unaccustomed to. I am compassionate to them yet I am unable to help them.

The time was 7.00 p.m.

An estimated crowds of 8,000 people filled the Indoor Stadium of Johor Bahru. I explained the meaning of True Buddha empowerment.

There are two important aspects of empowerment. The first is affirmation, and the second, guarantee. Empowerment is a special ritual in Tantra.

I also explained the true meanings of empowerment for the following :

(1) Vase
(2) Precious Crown
(3) Vajra
(4) Bell
(5) Name

After receiving all the five types of empowerment, a practitioner should have accumulated adequate virtue to understand the sequence of cultivation. If he has experienced Samadhi, a stage of tranquillity exempt from all external sensations, or enters into Vairocana's sea of lights, or contemplation of the five stages in Vairocana Buddhahood (entry into the Bodhi-mind, maintenance of it, attainment of the diamond mind, realization of the diamond embodiment, and perfect attainment of Buddhahood.) then he is qualified to inherit the tantra tradition and impart the acarya empowerment.

A true Vajra Guru is a person who has achieved a certain level of proficiency in his cultivation ; be it upper, middle or lower level. He is qualified to teach the empowerment rituals, as he has accumulated certain merit and is able to use certain mystic powers. Most important of all, he is well versed in the rites of empowerment. He knows how to invoke and embody the root deity of wisdom. The Vajra guru turns himself into Vajradhara whose task is to use Tantra to succour human beings.

A truly qualified Vajra Guru must have four pre-requisites:

1. His cultivation must reach certain level.
2. He must have mystic powers.
3. He must manifest his merit.
4. He must be able to embody Vajradhara.

Then his empowerment can be powerful and effective.

To receive empowerment, the disciples must:

1. Make a vow to learn Tantra whole-heartedly and with unceasing effort. Willing to be enlightened as a Buddha and return to succour others.

2. Have confidence in his guru, apart from knowing the basic theory on Sutrayana and Tantrayana.
3. Observe all the precepts, amongst others the 50 guru stanza; 14 root tantric precepts ; 5 precepts and 10 good deeds. Be willing to devote life, wealth, willpower, and time to the guru.
4. Master the sequence of cultivation. Always follow the guidance of the guru to do cultivation, never attempt any short-cut.

I will now teach you how to visualise different colours of light during empowerment :

1. White light is visualised for misfortune eradication.
2. Red light is visualised for loving kindness.
3. Yellow light is visualised for merit accumulation.
4. Blue light is visualised for demon subjugation.

If a disciple after receiving empowerment still encounters bad dreams at night, then obviously he did not receive the benefits from such empowerment. He must repent for his unwholesome karma by doing the confessional rites (ksamayati). He can ask the guru to empower him again once he started to have good dreams.

This is the only condition a disciple must have before receiving empowerment from the guru.

Geomancy

Note : In the first part of this article, Grandmaster talked about the geomancy of Da Guan Villa. As he quoted at length from classical chinese, and used Jargon to assess the well-being of the Villa, the translator is unable to decipher them yet. Regrets

I told the disciples of True Buddha School when I was at the Da Guan Villa:

"The knowledge of Geomancy is wide and profound. There are many and varied schools around. I have learned the "Nine Star tradition" from Qing Zhen the priest. The purpose of learning Geomancy is to change the fate of human beings; and carry out the salvation mission."

Armed with the knowledge of Geomancy is just like having two knives, I am able to go through fire and water to help the poor and the needy, to show my bold and uninhibited characters. In fact, I even thought of using geomancy to lead a vagrant life. To make my home wherever I am, and maintain an uncertain whereabouts.

The cream of geomancy once mastered will lead to instant results. Traditional knowledge of geomancy will need at least 3 to 5 years if not 10 years to master. Moreover we need to practise divination. The knowledge of geomancy must surely be fake if there is no success in our interpretations.

Since Qing Zhen the priest is the best in geomancy. My skills will never be too bad.

It is a pity that nowadays, most of the geomancy practitioners are without any lineage. With only a little knowledge, they just set up shop to mislead others. It is too bad!

A critic of an analogy by Xing Yun, the dharma master

Time : Noon

Date : December 21, 1992

Venue : Johor Bahru Airport

Cause : A lot of magazines and newspapers were given to me by the disciples from Da Guan Chapter. I found an interesting article which recorded the interview of Xing Yun, the dharma master. I reproduced it below:

Question: (by the reporter from China news.)

"Rev. Dharma master, what do you think of a monk who renounces his ordination?"

Answer : "It is an ordinary affair for the monk to renounce his ordination. Let me use an analogy, it is the same as a teacher who gives up teaching."

This analogy gave me an ever lasting impression. Although the level of achievement in Xin Yun's cultivation cannot be gauged outwardly, Sometimes his act showed his innocence; and his words indicated his ignorance.

I really admire his determination and courage to talk irresponsibly. I concede that Xing Yun has a disposition in his tyranny that impressed me very much. His sermons clearly showed his determination and courage.

Xing Yun has been in the religious fields for quite some time now. His great ambition can be gleaned from starting a new calendar and called it 26 years after the Buddha light era.

After observing him thoroughly, I think he could be the subjects of:

Wheeling and dealing
Seeking acquaintance
Love affairs
Politicking
Building a big temple

These are the five folklore of Xing Yun, the dharma master. Having the urge to write them, I exclaimed: "Such an interesting person like Xing Yun, the dharma teacher provides us with endless folklore. I just could not stop quoting him."

"Renouncing ordination is just like a teacher who gives up teaching", the analogy cautiously created by him sank me into a deep thought.

When a teacher gives up teaching:

He changes his job (common)
He retires because of old age (common)
He is not feeling well (common)

For a teacher to give up his teaching post, it is not a sensational news. There are so many such instances, I find it nothing unusual. Everybody knows when a teacher gets old, he looks forward to his retirement.

But when a monk renounces his ordination, can we use "teacher giving up teaching" as an analogy ?

Ordination is a life long commitment. You cannot change the job (usual)

Can the monks renounce their ordination when they get old ? (They can't)

Can the monks renounce their ordination when they are not feeling well ? (They can't)

Ordination is not a job. The monks must take vows to cultivate and succour other sentient beings. It demands quite an amazing willpower. How can it be compared with choosing a job. The monks value vows, whereas the teachers treasure the career. They can never be lumped together.

Some tasks are important while others are not. We cannot compare them. Becoming a monk is a life long affair, it is an important decision. Teaching is not so, we can change the job anytime we like.

They are not the same!

The analogy from Xing Yun shows the dharma master's ignorance and wild talk to the extreme. They are just a pack of lies. His reasoning power is equalled to zero. I wonder how qualified he is to succour other sentient beings.

I believe that if a dharma master who does not have a breakthrough in his thought, and be enlightened in the process, he is as good as a dead person. No matter how great his development plan is, how many temples he helped to build, how many disciples he has, at most he can be considered a parvenu who has accumulated billions of dollars of wealth in the process.

The analogy of Xing Yun results in a laughter, an applause, and my deep sigh.

Everything happening in this world will be a thing of the past in no time. I could only sigh and laugh at his analogy. Finding a pen, I recorded this interesting episode in my diary on the tour to Singapore and Malaysia.

An auspicious sign of hues of rosy clouds appearing in the sky

A beautiful rainbow appeared in the sky when we were at the Subang Airport on December 22, 1992, at about 9.00 a.m. Guru Lian Xiang, Guru Lian Zhi, Gao Cheng Zu and myself witnessed this auspicious sign.

It is inconceivable that whenever I visited a place, its sky will be surrounded by auspicious clouds and lights, coupled with radiating rainbows.

To many people, this is just an ordinary phenomena. To tell the truth, this is the congregation of Buddhas, Bodhisattvas and heavenly beings in Malaysia to welcome me. At that moment, many had heard music and drum beats from the sky, and smelled fragrance around the area but they just could not tell where they were from.

When I arrived at Penang, there were two rainbows in the sky. A rainbow bridge emerged on top of layers of clouds to welcome me in Brunei. Approaching Sibu, our plane had to pass through a rainbow. It is like heavenly beings using beautiful flowers to garland us. (Everybody just screamed at the sight.)

Three layers of rainbow appearing beside the moon, when I presided over a ritual at Tawau. During the empowerment session, the master of ceremony made an announcement. All the participants rushed out to see the spectacular sight; they felt very happy about it.

Hues of rosy clouds always appeared in the sky when I did the initiation rite on the images. The auspicious sign was so fascinating that some participants even saw the Buddhas and Bodhisattvas entering into their own images. The initiation rite was really effective ! The rosy clouds took many forms, sometimes they formed the shape of precious covers, stone pillars , auspicious lamps, flying dragons and lotus flowers.

The appearances of rainbows and other auspicious signs during my visit to Singapore and Malaysia further confirmed my uniqueness.

"Lu Sheng-Yen is one and only, " said many observers.

The first time Master Lu stepped in the capital of Malaysia, rainbow appeared in the sky, auspicious clouds gathered, followed by the congregation of Buddhas, Brahmas Indra, devas, nagas, yaksas, gandharvas, asuras, garudas, kinnaras, mahorogas and many others.

The Malaysian Newspapers even headlined: "Congregation of Buddhas and Gods." Surely all of them came to welcome me.

Like a tornado passing through Malaysia, Master Lu Sheng-Yen was able to attract more than 10,000 people to take refuge in him. The scene at the ceremony was so hot that it almost exploded.

When the wind subsided, the torpidity of Buddhism in Malaysia was given a new life. I used the dharma whip: to expose the minds of those fake dharma masters, to reveal their true colours.

(The dharma masters there were protecting their own resources, and found ways and means to consolidate their wealth. They went to court to fight for additional income. It is evident from the infighting between dharma masters Ji Chen and Shu Yi.)

Before my arrival, Buddhism in Malaysia was lackadaisical. It is filthy everywhere.

And now the wind suddenly stopped. The silence was broken by a bone-gnawing yellow dog dashing out from the bushes.

The dog was not barking at the other dogs. It was barking at me, a stranger - passing by.

I did not pay any attention to the dog, as it was just a blind dog that will bark at any body.

Living Buddha in Kuala Lumpur

Living Buddha Lian Sheng created a furore in Kuala Lumpur. Although staying in a presidential suite in Imperial Hotel, he only worn a faded red lama costume. He used an additional yellow pouch when he had to go out. He did not have other belongings apart from a hand luggage.

When he had nothing to do in the suite, he would pace up and down. His chanting was only broken by the noise made by the rosary beads he used. If he sat on the sofa, he would go into meditation. The hall was so quiet that a fallen needle would be heard clearly.

But a tornado was brewing in Kuala Lumpur. The signboard of Buddhism was blowing in the wind; it is just a matter of time it would drop off. A yellow dog was howling below the sign board. Its tune was hoarse, full of sorrow and short of breath.

Kuala Lumpur is the biggest and the most boisterous city in Malaysia. Many hawkers were doing business near the high-rise buildings. The cooking utensils used by the eating stalls could be heard from far. Noises from the passing vehicles, the nearby restaurants together with the laughter of the customers and the voices of singers were as glittering as the neon lights.

It is a prosperous city, an ultra modern one. Suddenly everyone in the city remembers an important date, i.e. December 26. This golden date is the most important date in their lives. They can unload the burden as heavy as a thousand kati. On this date, Master Lu Sheng-Yen will take the stage in Kuala Lumpur. Master Lu is a man of mystery, everybody will want to see him taking out his mask.

The yellow dog was clawing ahead, but its body was curving backward. When the day finally arrived, a lot of people converged at the national stadium. Few people went to the restaurants, or patronised the night spots. Even fewer people remained at home or wondered on the streets. They flocked at the stadium and listened to what Lu Sheng-Yen had to talk about "True Buddha."

Kuala Lumpur had never seen such a commotion before. The rising star in the religious world, Master Lu Sheng-Yen was making his first appearance in the capital of Malaysia.

All the newspapers in Kuala Lumpur made news of Master Lu Sheng-Yen their headlines. They devoted a big column to carry his news everyday. Master Lu Sheng-Yen stole the lime lights and was considered man of the hour.

Amongst others, were the following : Nanyang Shang Pao, Sin Chew daily, Sin Ming daily, The China press, Ming Sheng Pao, Tong Pao, New life press, Man weekly, Times.....Star (English medium). It is an assembly of news medium.

His exposure to the media was unrivalled:

The country's President could not match him. The Pope of catholicism trailed him. Even the popular film star seemed pale.

Residents of big city like Kuala Lumpur normally lead a stressful life. They will not be easily arose by whoever coming to town. They are quite numb in their feelings. But to their surprise, they are attracted by Lu Sheng-Yen, who command such a big following. He caught many by surprise.

I am not a native returning home, I am just a passer by.

As a traveller who passed by, I rekindled the light of traditional Buddhism which was once considered deserted and non- existence. I cleared away the spider webs and gave it a clean and refreshing look. The rusts were removed, the parts oiled, and the dust cleared.

We are from the True Buddha School which possesses all kinds of mystic powers. There is a causation for me to preach the True Buddha Tantra. The time is right and the place most suitable.

When Sakyamuni Buddha was born, he showed his mystic powers. He moved seven steps and formed seven lotus flowers. Pointing to the heaven and earth, he said: "I am the honoured one in the divine." When Jesus Christ was born, the star glittered and three learned men came to make offerings.

I was wearing a piece of white heavenly cloth when I was born.

The news travelled slowly, at its own pace, but those with sharp ears will hear about it; and talk about it. Soon, one will tell ten, ten will tell hundred, and soon the whole world will know about it.

Those cultivating True Buddha Tantra really have achieved spiritual response, we have witnesses and evidence to show. It is true and not fabricated by us.

A personal interview by ms Zhang Bi Fang

I was interviewed by Ms Zhang Bi Fang on December 24,1992 at 6:00 p.m. She is a well-known reporter from Man's weekly. I understand that she took up a law course at the same time and became a lawyer. She specialises in interviewing head of states.

Claiming to be a Buddhist, she wanted to interview me personally. I acceded to her request.

Round face, medium built, regular features, she created quite a good impression on me. She also displayed the typical characteristics of a lawyer: She is cool and steady; smart and outrageous.

Her charming and beautiful eyes have become sharp and piercing after prolonged practical training.

A war was waged.

She fired questions at me.

I responded immediately.

When I threw a question back to her, she could not answer.

Her face blushed; She became restless and uneasy.

She is a smart and stubborn woman who has gone through the thick and thin in life. She is charming and has a strong personal view. She can be more feminine than most women; occasionally she shows her masculine nature. She is more capable than most men.

When her article on me appeared in the Man's weekly, my photograph became the front cover. To tell the truth, her special feature did not impress me. She holds too strong a personal view that the interview turned out to be her personal vindication. And her style of writing was too defying. She is more a lawyer than a reporter.

The feminity of being smooth and tender was totally absent, she showed undaunted and relentless proficiency.

I wonder if she is really a Buddhist, as she made quite a few fundamental mistakes on Buddhist terms, for instance, the name of Yin Shun was written as Ying Shun (Yin Shun, a prolific writer considered the beacon and the most well-known teacher in Buddhism. What a pity, she did not know one of the teachers I took refuge in, obviously she never read his books.)

Moreover, in the two falsified sutras that I mentioned, she wrote the names wrongly. Three vehicles became three layers .... and many more mistakes.

She claimed to have followed the noble eightfold path. Maybe she did not know that when I explained the meaning of Heart Sutra at Lei Zhang Temple in Seattle, I spent more than three months to expound the concept of noble eightfold path. The concept was also scattered in the 104 books written by me.

1. Correct views.
   (understand the four noble truths)
2. Correct thought and purpose.
   (nurture right and eradicate false thoughts)
3. Correct speech
   (purify speech and avoid false talk)
4. Correct conduct
   (maintain best earthly behaviour and do ten good deeds.)
5. Correct livelihood
   (lead a normal life and distance from five improper ways of livelihood. Notes: the five improper ways of livelihood for a monk (1) changing his appearance (2) advertising his own powers and virtue (3) fortune-telling by physiognomy (4) hectoring and bullying (5) praising the generosity of another to induce the

hearer to bestow presents.)

6. Correct Zeal
   (put extra efforts in cultivating the right dharma)

7. Correct remembrance
   (have the spiritual response and do not mourn over gain and loss)

8. Correct meditation
   (be pure and intact)

In her article, she was everything but tender. Moreover she is impatient and short-tempered.

Personally, I believe:

As Buddhists, we must learn to be patient even under duress. We must see things from a broader perspective. We must not be hasty and hot-tempered in our writing, and jump to conclusions. By doing so, it will only create more unwholesome karma.

Security guards

The propagation tour to Kuala Lumpur was organised by the committee for propagation of True Buddha School of dharma in Kuala Lumpur, Selangor.

I wrote a verse to the committee:

Snowy (abbreviation for Selangor) mountain, the four religions converge into a mighty dharma current.

The only time it is flourishing (abbreviation for Kuala Lumpur) Doctrines of Mahayana and Hinayana school of Buddhism are spreading, And Tantra will be imparted like a rainbow in the sky.

Members of the organising committee are as follows:

Chairman : Gao Cheng Zhu
Vice Chairman : Luo Yi Ren
Treasurer : Ma Zhong Hua
Secretary : Li Zhu
Public Relation : Gu Yun
Members : Wan Xiu, Luo Wen Ying, Xie Te Ren,
Cheng Chih
Kua, Yie Mei Lan, Si Mei Ling
Guru In charge : Lian Zhi

Heads of sub committee :

Facilities : Luo Xi Quan
Shrine decoration : Zheng Zhi Kun
Sutra Recital : All disciples
Master of ceremony : Chai Chong Ren
Discipline : Wei San Lie
Distribution : Zhang Ting Zhong
Reception : Gu Yun
Photograph : Yie Jian Ming
Sound systems : Chen Sheng Rui
Public Relations : Li Zhu
First Aids : Luo Fa Zheng
Publication : Yuan Xiu
Offering : Yie Mei Lan
Transportation : Li Zhen Fu
Lion Dance : Luo Fa Zhang
Consultation : Lian Zhi
Correspondence : Wu En Hua
Hotel : Shi Mei Ling
Meal : Yang Ya Qiu
Security : Wang A Lie
Sarira : Tuo Sheng Xi
Special duty : Luo Wun Yin
Tour : Gu Yun

A special feature in the organising committee is that the security personnel consisted of twenty Malays who are dark and sturdy. (Ex-sharp shooters from the army) They dressed in dark suits, and kept their weapons around their waists- an eye catching lot. They followed me wherever I went. When I sat in front, they would be at the back and vice versa. They surrounded me in the lift. When I went to the toilet, they waited outside, no matter how long. When I ate my meal, they would stand behind me. During sleeping time, they would set up a table outside my room, and two sentries would be on duty in two hourly detail. It was a round-the-clock protection for me, I was never left alone.

They did not leave me out of sight even when I gave sermons at Dharma Shrine and Lian Yuan chapter on Christmas day.

They were as ready as ever. With penetrating eyes, they observed the crowds and dark corners, as if the surrounding was full of perils and crafty foxes. Whenever I stooped, they stooped too. When I stood, they did so.

I asked the reason for such a tight security arrangement. Someone told me privately, "Living Buddha Lian Sheng is like the sun at high noon. He is too popular. A local gangster is not too happy about this. He let out the news that he would punch the living Buddha in public, and have such photographs printed in the press, if Living Buddha

Lian Sheng were to come to Kuala Lumpur. His intention is to disgrace the Living Buddha-a cut above the others, into a worthless mouse."

The committee was very nervous on hearing the rumour.

A special security group was thus set up to protect me. On hearing this explanation, I felt :

"In a boring world, people tend to do meaningless acts. To be a well-known personality, one has to pay a high stake. Although he has a high social status, deep in his heart, he may feel empty, monotonous and lonely." It reminded me of the Living Buddha of Golden Hill. When he was still alive, many did not believe in him and treated him like an eyesore, and ridiculed him.

A manure bucket was even poured on his head to disgrace him. But Living Buddha Golden Hill did not stop hitting the wooden fish, as if nothing happened to him. Chanting the name of Amitabha Buddha, he walked away, faeces still on his head. Disgrace was nothing to him.

I wonder what would happen if the news of assault appeared in the press. I would not be frightened, I would not weep. But I cannot tell how pale I am and whether I could manage a reluctant smile. I do not know how I would react under such circumstance.

If I am battered to death,it would be an end albeit a speechless one.

I would be better off, if I survived. I could carry on my writing career.

The gathering at the National Stadium

$2$5,000 people attended the ritual held at the National Stadium, Kuala Lumpur, Malaysia on December 26, 1992 at 6.00 p.m.

China Press:

"The world renowned Vajra guru Master Lu Sheng-Yen conducted the most explosive ritual. A sea of people filled the spectacular show for calamity eradication, merit accumulation, souls' deliverance...."

Sin Chew Daily:

"Living Buddha Lian Sheng, a noted Buddhist master came to the Indoor Stadium of Kuala Lumpur to conduct a soul deliverance ritual. The grand occasion attracted a full crowd."

Nanyang Sang Pao:

"A full capacity crowd gathered at the stadium to listen to Living Buddha Lian Sheng's first propagation in Kuala Lumpur. He demonstrated the compassionate power of Buddhism."

Sin Ming Daily:

"Using mercy to influence others, he helps to

build a society full of peace and loving kindness."

Communication Press:

"Buddhism has become part of our life....,
purification of human minds and encouraging them
to do good deeds..., more than 20,000 people
participated."

Just before 6 O'clock in the evening, the biggest
indoor stadium in Malaysia was already filled to
capacity, even the corridors and steps were occupied.
Latecomers had to stand outside after the iron gate
was closed. More than 25,000 people participated in
the ritual and 5,000 of them took refuge there and
then.

Officially declared open jointly by Deputy
Finance Minister Dato Lu Ying You, and members
of parliament cum Malaysia Chinese Association
Chairman at self-governed district, Mr Chen Chai
He, the ritual was an exceptionally grand occasion.

Big stadium, high roof, long steps, thousand
lamps, males and females, young and old ; what a
fantastic sight!

"May all of you be well!" I said.

"Same to you, Grand master! " the crowd replied.

My throat was choked, I was unable to utter a
word. The crowd remained silent. The time had

stopped to facilitate the exchange of our feelings and thoughts.

During the ritual, many of them wept uncontrollably. Not that they were sad, injured or broken-hearted, they shed the tears of joy. The tears from the men, and women whether young or old were equally crystal-clear and glittering like the morning dew.

With radiating vigour, I started to deliver my sermon.

Once I started to speak, many people took refuge.

I talked about the truths in True Buddha School.

The truth in its pure land- Maha Double Lotus Pond.

The truth in my reaffirmation as a Buddha by Sakyamuni Buddha.

The truth in my cultivation with unceasing efforts and experiencing real manifestations.

The truth in Tantra, a true Buddhist dharma.

The truth in manifestation and knowing the level of achievement in my cultivation.

I had been to Maha Double Lotus Pond and saw my dharma body to be Padmakumara. This encounter is not fabricated. I have vowed that if this is a lie I shall be doomed to Avici hell (suffering without interval), and never be given a chance for transmigration.

Using my life, my full vitality, my unrivalled confidence, my sincere heart, my true realization, I guarantee that all of you will be reborn in the Buddha Pure Land and be enlightened as a Buddha, as long as you respect your teachers, treasure the dharma and cultivate personally.

The gathering at the Indoor Stadium was just like that of Spirit Vulture Peak.

It is said, "That Living Buddha Lian Sheng though exquisite, is capable of numerous changes."

"When Living Buddha Lian Sheng opens his mouth, many will take refuge. When he speaks again, even more will be enlightened."

"The articles written by Living Buddha Lian Sheng is peerless."

I say it is too early yet. I shall impart the oral traditions of Tantra to the whole world at an opportune time. I shall use the fastest and most effective way to succour human beings.

My ultimate aim in life is none other than :

"Achieve self realization. And help others to gain enlightenment. And finally reach a perfect stage in cultivation."

I do not mobilize the crowd, nor do I be subservient to them. It is not a kingdom of religions.

I do it naturally without any hidden agenda.

When I am old, many people will be puzzled by my act. For I, Living Buddha Lian Sheng, will retire by throwing away all the fame and status achieved. I shall not attach to anything, for I have nothing. I shall be alone, may be accompanied by a lamp and a bed.

Batu Cave (Black Wind Cave)

On a windy and drizzling day, we visited the Batu Cave. As the name implies, it is a cave on top of a hill. We had to climb a long and steep flight of steps to reach the top, which is wide enough to hold more than a thousand people.

A Hindu temple is built there. The lamps brighten up the place. Mahabrahman is the creator of universe; and the main god worshipped by the Hindu. With four arms and four faces, his image shows him wearing a crown, and sitting on a seven-geese wagon.

Another image is Yamadevaloka, who is in charge of the nether world. His image sits on a water Buffalo, with his right hand holding a human skull and his left palm facing upwards. And two heavenly girls in attendance.

There is also an image of Sarasvati. On the his left is the image of Goddess Piniu, who holds a lute in her left hand and plays with her right hand. She is also known as Goddess of Mystic sound.

I saw the image of Isvaradeva, the main god of Hindu. He is the valiant Siva who rides on a black and greenish water buffalo.

I also saw garuda ridden by Narayana-deva, and Ganesa, the elephant head fortune god ....

These images of Hindus symbolize the vibrating life and the culmination of human spirit.

The cave was spacious. We strolled from the front to the back and made our journey back quietly. We did not utter a word as this was the sacred place for the Hindus.

We could not stop showing our respect and admiration once we stepped inside the cave. The images of the gods were vigorous and nimble and the images of the goddess showed the ability to sing, dance, drink and play the instruments.

(In fact, Buddhism originated from Hinduism. Buddha lived under the strong influence of Hinduism. The four noble truth, the twelve nidanas (chain of existence), the noble eightfold path, the three signs of Hinayana (i.e. Non-permanence, Non-personality, and Nirvana), the law of Karma, all showed traces of Hinduism. Even the heavens mentioned in Buddhism were borrowed from Hinduism.)

Sakyamuni Buddha at first practised Asceticism at the snowy mountain for six years. He was cultivating the ascetic meditation taught by the Hindu deities.

Later on, when Sakyamuni Buddha gained his enlightenment, he founded Buddhism.

To many Indians, Buddhism is just a branch of Hinduism that went on to become a new religion.

What a coincidence ! We saw the fire Puja ritual of Hinduism being held at the entrance to the cave. All the priests did not wear their tops when they recited prayers and chanted mantra, to the accompaniment of musical instruments. They put their offerings into the fire.

One of the older priest who had a loud voice, was seen to be moving forward and backward, with his body twisting and turning. All the believers seated silently in front of the altar. They were all Indians. The females dressed in sarong, with a cinnabar dot between their eyebrows.

As we moved closer to them, they knew we were Buddhist monks, since we were cleanly shaved and wore lama costumes. But they did not mind.

I have conducted many fire puja in my life. But this is the first time I saw a fire puja of Hinduism dedicated to the heaven. I was nervous, excited and enthusiastic. I stayed there from the beginning of the ritual right to the end.

As an expert, I could feel the heavenly beings coming to receive their offerings. My spiritual response was definitely right.

Living Buddha Lian Sheng concedes: "Hinduism has its mystic powers. So are the prayers of Christianity, Catholicism, and Islam. All of them have mystic powers."

Facing the sky, I took a deep breath. Although there is only one sky, we have prejudice because of the different faiths. The prejudice of revelation of the whole or the part, complete enlightenment or partial. The difference lies in the level of achievement, although the apex is one and the same. Sakyamuni Buddha is an enlightened one, since he made a distinction between functional and perfect teaching, expediency and reality, normal unenlightened ideas and sacred dogmas.

As an enlightened person, I know everything. I am able to endure all kinds of slander and insults.

The mist at Genting Highlands

We went up to Genting Highlands on December 27, 1992, at 6.00 p.m. by bus.

Genting Highlands, a casino and a place of interest, is not only vigorous but also energetic. The weather is cool and the view spectacular.

As a non-gambler, I did not bring a big stake there. Moreover I could not guarantee that I would win.

In fact, I always advise people not to gamble. Why ? No matter how much you eat, you drink, you play, you enjoy, there is a limit to the expenditure incurred. But it is not so if you indulge in gambling, there is no limit to the loss.

Few people can be saved from this vice. A compulsive gambler is willing to die for the cause, knowing that it is a fire pit, and be prepared to jump into it, as if the death will be a comfortable one.

The entrance of the casino as designed by a noted geomancy master, is of the shape of an eagle claws. On passing through the roof, the eagle can snatch your wealth away. And the loot will be given to the casino owner. His fortune is derived from the customers' misfortune.

It is said the main entrance is guarded by many child ghosts, who can suck away your gambling luck. Without such luck, the gamblers will surely lose.

The casino is located on the first floor, so if you take escalator up, you are warned not to touch the handrails as your good hands will be taken away by the child ghosts .

As gamblers believe in "luck and good hands", these are taboos for them.

As far as I am concerned, the ending will always be the same. You will be ripped off and become a loser, whether your luck is good or not, you are kind or unkind, courageous or otherwise. There is no difference for a saint and a commoner, a hero and a coward. The casino owner will always be the winner, that is why the casino is doing a thriving business.

The road leading to Genting Highland is winding and built around the hills. Seen backward, the road looks like a river with nine turns, the sight is spectacular.

As the road is very narrow and the ascendence can be quite steep at times, the vehicle takes a heavy beating.

Winding rivers, steep cliff and boundless greenery appear from both sides of the road from time to time. As we climbed higher, the greenery became more gaudy. More and more primitive trees met our eyes. The air was even more soothing; we really enjoyed our breathing. The landscape was really "edible".

As we continued our journey, we passed through layers of clouds. No wonder, the place is known as Genting (On top of the cloud in Mandarin).

Touring a stupa and a temple on our way to the peak, we saw only mist on reaching our destination, instead of the casino and the lake. The mist was so thick that we could not even see the nearby lake. In fact we saw nothing at all.

I presumed the lake must be as sparkling as a pearl. And the water in it deep blue and transparent. The fresh air and colourful flower beds made the place ostentatious. At night, the neon lights will brighten the garden, and the willow will dance gracefully and there will be many tourists around.

The building is very modern. Apart from hotel rooms, it has restaurants, amusement park, casino, health club,.......

The scenery must be eye-catching. What a pity we could not see the big and grand garden with its pavilions, since the thick mist was accompanied by strong winds and occasional showers.

No green green grass of land, no boundless lake that is full of water.

Genting Highlands is well-known though we did not come to gamble.

Dressed in Lama costumes and incense pouches around our necks, we came to see the beautiful scenery, to breathe the fresh air. To our disappointment, we saw only the mist.

I contend, "Mist is after all a good thing. It is simple and yet typical. It is light and full of simplicity and dignity." "Enjoying the care-free mist is like comprehending the misted heart in a bewildering world leisurely."

The charm of Butterflies

I wrote a book "The charm of Butterflies" previously.

Flying from Kuala Lumpur to Penang on December 28, 1992, I visited the Butterfly garden at 3:00 p.m.

I enjoyed the charm of butterflies from a close distance. They stuck out their tongues to lick the pineapple juice. The tongue is black, thin and as long as its body. I came to realize the analogy of long-tongue woman to a beautiful butterfly.

During the visit, I must have seen more than a thousand species of butterflies. The world of butterflies must be more complicated than that of the mankind, I believe.

Their skills in camouflaging surprised me. They are able to adapt to their surroundings by changing their colours, so that they cannot be detected by their enemies.

Some of the butterflies are able to rest between the leaves and the branches. And the colours of their clothes (wings) are almost the same as the surrounding leaves.

Hanging between branches, some butterflies look

more like dry twigs. Unless you pay special attention, you cannot tell whether they are twigs or butterflies.

Some butterflies attach their bodies to the stone and the shape of the stone is identical to that of the butterflies. The butterflies have embodied the stone; they are one and the same.

Slumbering in the sand pitch are some butterflies that have sand- like wings. They look just like a heap of sand from afar, it is not easy to spot them.

"Butterflies are like Ninjas, who are capable of disguising themselves into many things."

I watched closely how a caterpillar changed into a pupa, then into a butterfly. The world of butterflies is really eventful.

Suddenly I burst into laughter. Why? I concluded that "Those who fear death, are in fact dying faster." The life of a butterfly is never long; after a few dances, it will be dead. And yet the butterflies are so afraid to die. Normally all animals are master of their own lives. Only the butterflies are unable to protect themselves when they are attacked; they try their best to protect themselves though.

My first impression was that they would be warriors capable of going through fire and water, and they will never be afraid of death. They will not be threatened by death when they enjoy collecting the nectar from the flowers. But I was wrong. While enjoying, they fear death also. In fact they faked death.

I have to conclude that the charm of butterflies lies in their enjoyment, not when they are under attack.

I will still be a warrior to walk the road of no return. I have vowed that "Risking my life and breaking my bones, I will succour all human beings." I really understand the enjoyment of life and the fear of death.

To die for Buddhist dharma is glorious. My eyes will show the spirit of fearlessness. To propagate the True Buddha Tantra, I am not scared of death, as long as I can succour a few more human beings.

With this state of mind, I set out to succour human beings. I have a lot of problems, but I am not bothered by them, as I know the right time to pass my life to the cosmic power.

I concede, "Life and death are so swift both to the butterflies and to the human beings. It is better to be a hero than a coward in your life time."

The path of cultivation is the most lofty and the most valuable. Only through personal cultivation can life be meaningful. All other ways are but a dead end. The path of cultivation is the only way leading to the truth. Only those who are wise enough, rational enough, learned enough, and have the right causation can follow this unparalleled path.

The temple at the middle section of the hill-Kek Lok Si

How can I not visit Kek Lok Si when I am in Penang ? Buddhism is thriving in Penang. Kek Lok Si is a temple that was set up by Miao Lian the Abbot of "Yong Chuan Shi" at Fu Zhou's Drum Hill, when he came to Penang.

The top disciple of Miao Lian was Xu Yun the elderly monk, who had great causation with the temple. He gave sermons on Lotus Sutra at the Kek Lok Si.

Xu Yun lived for 120 years. Apart from being the National teacher in Ching Dynasty, he is still considered a spiritual leader of contemporary Buddhism.

Xu Yun's life was full of saga. He became a monk when he was nineteen. He put in painstaking effort for three years at the back of "Yong Chuan" temple. He then spent three years walking from "Pu Tuo" mountain to "Wu Tai" mountain. (A bow after every three steps taken.) When he was forty eight, he toured the world to meet all the noted teachers. Xu Yun is known to have a profound meditation skills, he could sit for nine days to half a month in a single meditation session. The famous stories about him, among others, included :

"Praying for rain fall at the Sleeping Dragon Temple."

"Stone moved by cloud."

"Meditation at Long Chuan temple."

"Animals taking refuge."

"Blossom of Iron tree."

"Meeting Meitreya Buddha."

Xu Yun and my teacher Dao An dharma master had good causation. The poem Xu Yun wrote after gaining enlightenment impressed me very much.

"When the cup is dropped, the dropping sound can be heard vividly; When emptiness is destroyed, the crazy heart can be stopped instantly."

Xu Yun encountered all kinds of hardship when he started to build ancestor courtyards for Zen Buddhism, those completed included:

Yun Qi Si at Ji Zhu Hill

Yong Chuan Si at Drum Hill

Nan Hua Si at Cao Xi

and Da Jue Si at Yun Men

Xu Yun had set up a college to teach Buddhism in Yong Chuan Si at Drum Hill, Fu Zhou. And Yin Shun was the great teacher, who was the first person I took refuge in.

I heard that Yin Shun stayed at the Kek Lok Si once. Bai Shen Dharma Master also stayed at the Kek Lok Si before. How can I not visit the temple?

I recalled Xu Yun's poem:

Passing through the "kong Tong mountain" Breaking a hole in the cloud, a road passes through, The meditation room seems far in the evening glows. The mountain is cold, as the rocks are covered with snow, When the moon touches the heart in meditation, the five skandhas (aggregates) will be empty. The stubborn stone blocks the smoke preventing us from return to the pristine. In the evening, the rain washes the Kong tong mountain. The monk cannot recall what he was asked, as he heard Kuang Zhen has a wind of Tao.

As we walked up the path way to Kek Lok Si, we had to climb many steps. I recited "Namo Amitabha" for each step I took. The sun was still very high in the sky. I did prostration in each and every of the following places: the new main hall under construction, the old main hall, front court, backyard. While thinking of the virtues that the ancients possessed, I had all sorts of feelings dwelling in my mind.

The image of Avalokitesvara Bodhisattva in Kek Lok Si is very well-known. I went through the door,

Da Xiong Hall, Left and Right pavilions, drum pavilion to visit Avalokitesvara Hall, Meitreya Hall, Isvara Hall, Virtue Hall, and Grand master Hall. I even walked pass dining room,lecture room, meditation room, monk cell. And I paid special attention to the rhythm of wood beaten by the monks.

Kek Lok Si was built in the middle section of the hill. It is a large temple that has a neoclassical style. It is one of the best in Penang. the surroundings are quite good. The only setback is too many visitors may affect the people doing cultivation there. In a modern country, it is a special feature to have beggars asking for money along the footpaths.

Thomas Gao drove the car, and "Tian Hua" chapter's Lian Yi guided me to tour the Kek Lok Si.

Lian Yi told me: "Tian Hua Chapter is just situated at the foot of the same hill."

I replied, "Such a good causation!"

I paid a courtesy call to Kek Lok Si because I admired the steadfast and persevering cultivation of Xu Yun the elderly monk, his distance from fame and wealth, his lofty filial piety, his faithful heart, and the righteous cause to protect the religion and dharma, his attention on education of monks, his profound stage of meditation, and his impartiality towards dharma......

It also reminded me the monk's character and his thoughts. I really admired his personal cultivation effort--- without taking a break for few decades. Relying on the Zen principle to handle affairs, his patience and perseverance are unparalleled. Even when he walked, slept, sat and moved, he was able to show his understanding on the path.

I recalled the five-word poem written by Xu Yun: "Staying in the mountain, my thought floated afar, Let alone, I am able to understand the boundlessness, The root of pine tree is my pillow, Only awakening to make my own tea."

In Penang, I also toured the snake temple, the bridge, attended opening ceremony and a dinner hosted by disciples.

And I stayed at the presidential suite of Pearl Hotel.

I would like all of you to share my deep feelings after visiting the Kek Lok Si temple. To me, the most valuable thing in this world is the word "spirit".

A sermon given to 8,000 people

Time : 7:00 p.m.
Date : December 29, 1992
Venue : Penang "De Jiao Hui"
Crowd : 8,000 people
Sermon : "The transformation of Greed, hatred, ignorance and grudge "
Speaker : Living Buddha Lian Sheng

Buddhism thrives in Penang amongst the Malaysian States. Previously when "Xu Yun" the elderly monk presided over one of the biggest rituals in Penang, many buddhists heard the news and they came from countries as far as Thailand, Burma and Laos. Together with many Malaysian Buddhists, about 5,000 people attended the function.

An ordinary dharma master will be able to draw a crowd of 500 to 600 people to a dharma talk.

"Xing Yun" the dharma master from Taiwan did draw about 2,000 people. But today, when Living Buddha Lian Sheng came to Penang, there was as many as 8,000 people. Did you expect that to happen ? What is the difference between Lu Sheng-Yen and the rest ?

An ordinary dharma master will have to take a

long time to arrange for such ritual, among others it calls for aggressive publicity and detailed planning.

But Living Buddha Lian Sheng came almost single-handedly, with little luggage to this small island, and yet he was able to draw 8,000 people to his sermon. Where did the crowds come from ? The Buddhism fraternity was shocked. Views are varied.

"Master Lu Sheng-Yen is considered the modern version of Sakyamuni Buddha by his disciples."

"One and only."

"How many master Lu are there in this world?"

"One only."

"In this world, people like Master Lu are few and far apart. If you miss the chance to listen to his dharma talk, you will regret for life."

The traditional Buddhism fraternity in Malaysia paid great attention to the movement of Master Lu Sheng-Yen. Why ? Because he heralded in a great enterprise in Buddhism. He is more capable than XXX the dharma master when he was in his forties. If the trend continues, very soon the Buddhism world will be under his control. Clinching their fists, showing eagle like aggressive eyes, they preyed on Master Lu like an animal. They made use of local newspaper-Brightness Daily to run articles from "I love my teacher-Master Lu Sheng-Yen", and "How I withdraw myself from True Buddha School."

Behaving like demons, they tried to use these two books that slandered me to trap me like their prey. But to no avail; these two books were useless.

"I love my teacher-Master Lu Sheng-Yen", was totally destroyed by another book "A love letter to a monk."

And, "How I withdraw myself from True Buddha School", has been thoroughly refuted by Guru Lian Han. Like a wolf, the Buddhism fraternity tried to finish Master Lu off. Unfortunately, the wolf was killed immediately, its brain crushed, its blood splashed.

The Malaysian Buddhism Fraternity intended to stop Master Lu's propagation tour. They wanted to chop his head off in the first instance. They prepared all kinds of written materials and made the first move. From Kuala Lumpur, they posted the two books mentioned to Deputy Finance Minister Dato Lu Yin Yu and Malaysian Chinese Association Chairman of self-governed district Mr Chen Chai He, and warned them by phone not to attend the ritual. They thought the blow would be fatal. But "The ritual at Kuala Lumpur was attended by 25,000 people." "Penang-8,000 people." They witnessed the success of the rituals; and Master Lu got away scot-free. They could not do a thing. The information they gathered was inaccurate and useless. And the counter publicity was effective and the function became even more successful.

Although Malaysia is a place full of murderous motives, Master Lu is cool, sharp and patient. He is a peculiar person. He knows how to use "four teals to counter a thousand kati ". The Malaysian Buddhism fraternity became a shit-eating dog, and was compelled to suffer in silence.

One dharma master (Guan XXX) said in remorse, "By attacking Lu Sheng-Yen, it turned out we are giving him opportunity to mount a counter publicity. The result is everybody knows about his presence. Out of curiosity, they went to his ritual to see him in person. The rituals conducted by us by far drew lesser people when compared with that done by Lu Sheng-Yen. I think we are useless, may be we should take refuge in True Buddha School. The traditional form of Buddhism is too senile; like an ugly old lady, unwanted any more." He sighed after saying this.

In Penang's sermon, I stressed:
  "Greed" to be transformed into "Buddha."
  "Hatred" to be transformed into "Vajra."
  "Ignorance" to be transformed into "Bodhisattva."

and "Grudge" to be transformed into "Treasure."

"We must not be afraid of greed, hatred, ignorance and grudge, we must transform them. Tantra teaches us to transfer our human nature into Buddha nature and be enlightened as a Buddha within our life ."

The scene at the dharma talk was never so grand before. The participants clapped their hands, paid respects to grand master, felt extremely happy and even shed the tears of joy.

They praised the well-conducted sermon and the ritual venue that is full of dharma bliss.

Since the sermon was so touching, the news travelled wide and far. Everybody knew about it. People in Penang had never seen anything like that before. The sight was so magnificent when many people took refuge during empowerment ceremony. They lined up orderly. They walked and knelt. They waited for their turns to see Living Buddha Lian Sheng personally.

Altogether 8,000 people sang the "guru heart Mantra" and recited "Namo Amitabha."

Overcoming the black magic

It is a well-known fact that people in Thailand and Malaysia practise Black Magic.

Lu Sheng-Yen is a household name. His disciples who worship him will enshrine his photograph and cultivate the Tantra - "Guru Yoga". When they see him, they will kneel down and prostrate to him, to show their utmost respect. In their eyes, Lu Sheng-Yen is a Buddha.

For those who oppose him, or become jealous of him, the appearance of Lu Sheng-Yen will blunt their popularity. They will find Lu Sheng-Yen disgusting. In short, there are people who have the greatest esteem for him; and there are people who want him dead.

It is thus ,not surprising for those who practise black magic to make an attempt on his life, to finish him off with a fatal strike.

The head of Lu Sheng-Yen must be the most valuable one in this world. Once the news that Lu Sheng-Yen has been killed by a head-hunter got around, the sorcerer will be even more popular. The problem is he must have unrivalled talent in order to deal with Lu Sheng-Yen, otherwise it will be a futile effort.

As I went to bed in the presidential suite of Pearl Hotel, Penang that night, I smelled a strange fragrance.

"Here they come", I told myself. I could see things others could not see; and I could feel things that others could not feel.

About ten child-ghosts that looked like demons lied in wait for me. Their hairs were sticking out in all directions, and shinning like a golden light. Their eyes were as stern as a wolf. Their snow-white teeth were as sharp as thorns, and their bites could kill a healthy cow instantly. Like demons, they closed in from all directions. In no time, they surrounded my bed. With a sad and shrill cry, the ten child-ghosts pounced on me like hungry wolves.

Imagine, a person being attacked by ten child-ghosts at once. Before he can scream, his neck may be broken, his heart pulled out, his blood splashed, and his bones crushed; he could be dead in seconds even if he is a healthy man.

This is Black magic. From nowhere the ten child-ghosts appeared, they surrounded you like a net. Once they tightened the net, you will be dead. This was a golden opportunity for the sorcerer who wanted to kill Lu Sheng-Yen. Lu Sheng-Yen was sure to die as he stayed motionless.

Sleeping in gentle and cultivated pose, I took a deep breath, and changed myself into a Vajra. I visualized myself turning into a Vajra by reciting the three syllable brightness Mantra "Lang, Yang, Kang."

Remaining in my bed, I did not move, nor did I get up and run away hastily. In fact, I did not step up my defence. At that precious last moment, the sound "Ka cha, Ka cha," could be heard vividly. Maybe Lu Sheng-Yen's neck was broken, his arms, legs and fingers were all bitten into pieces.......... Tragedies occurred in this world quite often, but wonderful things always befell on Master Lu Sheng-Yen. He was still perfectly alright in his bed. The first "Ka cha, Ka cha," was the sound made by the broken teeth of the first child-ghost; and the second "Ka cha, Ka cha," was the sound made by the broken teeth of the second child- ghost. In fact, all the ten child-ghosts had their teeth broken into pieces.

I knew they were the most proficient man-eaters. They had attacked many people and their victims appeared to have died of heart attacks. They have never failed so far. They never show sympathy as they are loyal to their master who commands them.

They were unhappy to have met their Waterloo; they screamed as they lost all their teeth. Their target was Lu Sheng-Yen, the one and only Lu Sheng-Yen. If Lu Sheng-Yen can be killed by Black Magic, then he should not be called Lu Sheng-Yen.

Black magic is strange and surreptitious. So is my Tantra. It is very difficult if not impossible to explain.

This chapter is about overcoming the black magic that took place in Penang. The saga is admired and well-liked by all my disciples.

The "Dharma Wheel" Fa Lun Chapter in Kuching

I flew from West Malaysia's Penang to East Malaysia's Kuching on December 30, 1992.

When I saw Lian Fu using a microphone to direct True Buddha disciples to sing the guru Mantra outside the airport, a tender feeling filled my heart. The chapter head Lian Hua Wen Kui came personally to welcome me too.

Kuching is the biggest city in East Malaysia. The word Kuching means cat. It is also known as the city of cats.

On the way to Dharma Wheel chapter, we had to pass through many straight thoroughfares that are lined by trees. The houses are few and dispersed. Although the sky was blue, the grass green and the air refreshing, a tourist visiting for the first time will soon find out that the biggest city in East Malaysia is just a sparsely populated village.

East Malaysia prefers to remain undeveloped than modernize to a cosmopolitan structure. Resettlement from West Malaysia is not welcomed. As the central government has no jurisdiction here, the immigration authority can act independently. We were very confused by the terms Sarawak and Borneo, since East Malaysia has many jungles and swampy lands. There are many True Buddha chapters in West Malaysia. Among the oldest chapters formed in East Malaysia are:

Dharma Wheel chapter - Kuching
Miao Li chapter - Sibu
Wan Fa chapter - Miri
Ben Que chapter - Sabah
Lei Zhang temple - Sabah
Lei Zhang temple - Lian Hu Tawau
Ren Shan chapter - Sandakan
Even Brunei is found in this big island.

Studying land-survey in my younger days, I know apart from jungles and swamp-lands, there are many rivers in this island. As the timber trade is thriving, the town is built along the river. There are departmental stores,government offices,cinemas hospital and shops in the business centre. The weather is rather hot; only cooler after a shower, but the tanned residents are full of hospitality. Apart from timber, East Malaysia is also endowed with natural resources such as tin, petrol etc..... Explorers and traders from all over the places were the early immigrants; Indonesians and Filipinos can still be found in many towns in East Malaysia. They speak

116

different languages and wear different costumes. The aborigines are Dayaks, Ibans and others.

At the Dharma Wheel chapter, I explained the meaning of the name of the chapter. I wanted the dharma wheel to be turned faster and more often. The sermon given by the Buddha is able to tame the evil forces, and this is the meaning of Wheel. As the sermon is never a standstill; passing from one person to another like a wheel, it is known as the dharma wheel.

The following quotation shows the meaning of dharma wheel: "The right view of non-birth heralds in a system to be emulated, this is dharma. Spreading to many and not to one person only, this is a wheel."

The three signs of dharma wheel that we always make reference to are:

1. Right view, right thought, right zeal, and right remembrance are the spoke of a wheel.
2. Right speech, right deed, and right livelihood are the hub of a wheel.
3. Correct meditation is the axle of a wheel.

(The authenticating object of my lineage given by my teacher, guru Tu Den Da Ji of the Gelugpa tradition is a dharma wheel made of diamonds.)

I said before:

"True Buddha Tantra is a righteous dharma."

"Many True Buddha disciples will have great attainment in their cultivation; as are evidenced by many who had sarira found in their remains."

"True Buddha Tantra consists of outer, inner, Tantra and profound Tantra. And the Tantra can be further classified into Practice, action, Yoga and the most profound sections."

I hope all the True Buddha disciples have full confidence in their cultivation. They must not be too enthusiastic and passionate like a person falling in love at first sight, only to cool off later or worse still, give up the faith.

Buddha said before, "Those who can maintain their first vow, will surely be enlightened as a Buddha."

The future of True Buddha School in Malaysia is very bright. The salvation mission is deep-rooted, encouraging, upright and eternal.

Those who are jealous of our success, concoct all kinds of rumours and laugh at our sufferings will be defeated eventually. Wherever Lu Sheng-Yen goes, the flowers will surely blossom!

The native head-hunter

December 30, 1992, 7 o'clock in the evening, we flew to Sibu from Kuching.

The chapter head of Miao Li chapter-Sibu, Mr Mao Qi Kui, arranged for us to see a dance performed by the aborigines of Borneo. The musical instruments used by them are drums and Gongs. I noticed their dances had three features:

1. Steps taken during the dance.
2. Signs formed by hands and fingers.
3. Twisting of their bodies.

Like a fashion parade, every race showed its own traditional costumes. Although the movement was simple and the degree of difficulty was not great, the dances were lively and relaxed; and left on me a lasting impression. Based on the festival dates, the dances centred around:

1. New year
2. Harvest
3. Offering to gods

One of the dances performed was very unique. It depicted an Iban Hero head-hunting. Armed with knife and spear, he killed a stranger and cut his head off. He then sang and danced with his loot. A young Iban girl was very impressed by his heroism, and decided to marry him.

Mao Qi Kui told me:

Amongst the aborigines of Borneo, there are many head-hunters who believe that,

1. The head of a stranger can be used as a foundation for a new bridge, this is to ensure that the bridge will be firm, guarded and will be not ruined.

2. By hanging as many strangers' heads as possible outside one's house, one's ancestors will be honoured. Head-hunting is therefore sacred and most respectable.

3. By offering stranger's head to the god as sacrifice , the god will be happy and the weather will be favourable.

4. A male will hang the heads he hunted on his neck to show his prowess so that he can attract beautiful woman to marry him. A female would like to marry a man who has hunted many heads.

Mao Qi Kui also told me:

The early immigrants of Borneo had to risk their lives. They may not return safely. Once, all the heads of people in an entire village were hunted by head-hunters. On hearing this, I used my hand to feel whether my head is still intact.

My view on head-hunting is as follows:

Human nature and animals' killer instincts are more or less identical. Long time ago, when civilisation had not appeared, the world was full of darkness everywhere. Human beings were barbaric. "The law of evolution",and "the fittest survives" were the order of the early human history.

Human beings enjoyed seeing others' defeats. They attacked their enemies with deep-rooted hatred. Killing others is a victory; and cutting their heads a symbol of success. They killed a person whom they did not know with arrows, knives and spears cold-bloodedly. This is a strange psychology.

They enjoy their own laughter and do not care about others' woes. The stranger deserves to be killed; it is not sinister, just a reflection of human nature. They subscribe to a purely imaginary myth and do not have any guilt with regards to cold-blooded murder. As a result, slaughtering was allowed to be carried out, many headless corpses, heads splashed with fresh blood were left to accompany the cold howling wind.

Did the killer have such a deep hatred towards his victim this life ? The answer is definitely no. There are many kinds of people in this world, male and female, young and old, living in different parts of the world and following different customs. And accordingly they use different killing methods. If you happen to meet one of them, you will be killed.

To an aborigine who meets a stranger, his only thought is "It is fate, I can't do a damn." Although he is poor, he will be well respected, and be admired by many young girls as he has hunted many heads. He has to sharpen his knife, his spear and be good with his bow and arrows. He must be strong enough to protect his woman, so that she can smile and enjoy a good night's sleep. If he is too weak, he will be killed. If he is too kind, he will also be killed. He is fated not to resist any violence.

My only regret is:

although the society has changed, barbarism is replaced by civilisation, the ways of life and the customs are still varied - -the killing methods have taken on different forms. I wonder if the strive for supremacy of human race has been annihilated from this world, or simply assumes another form in order to survive.

Eating Durian in Sibu

I ate durian for the first time when I was in Hong Kong.
(**My feeling** : such a sting and inedible fruit.)

The second time, I ate durian was at Guru Yang Zhong Chi's house in Malaysia.
(**My feeling:** if I am given a treat, I may take a seed or two. But I will never buy them.)

The third time I ate the fruit was at Guru Yang Zhong Chi's "Da Guan" Villa in Malaysia.
(**My feeling** : so, so.)

The fourth time, I gave a treat at the foot of Genting Highland, Malaysia.
(**My feeling** : it was OK.)

I took durian for the fifth time when I was in Sibu.
(**My feeling** : I should eat it every night.)

I believe that eating durians can be a compulsive habit now.

In Sibu, we went to the night bazaar near the market every night. The fruits were hung for sale; one of the stores was selling fresh durians. I learned to use my nose to choose a good durian. I told them I would treat them.

We ordered the durians by lots. We ate those good ones and kept the not-so-good ones for durian cakes. This way of buying was definitely more expensive.

The twinkling lights from nearby clearly showed my ugly look. My hands and my mouth were full of durian flesh, and my whole body smelled of durian, I looked as greedy as a hungry ghost.

A person's behaviour can be seen clearly when he eats durians.

It's said that the durians from Malaysia are both fragrant and sweet. They are the best but are not for export. Whereas durians from Thailand are sweet but have no fragrance; these durians are meant for export.

I am also told the durians from Malaysian are picked up from the ground when they ripened; those from Thailand are plucked from the trees.

When the durians are in season, the head of the family who is the sole bread-earner and the house-wife who controls the household expenses will pawn their valuables to buy durians if they are short of cash. The lure of durians is very great, I notice those who like durians, their mouths water when the word durian is mentioned.

How is the durian tastes like ?

Lian Man and Chang Ren ran far far away.

But Chang Zhi smiled, his saliva dripping.

Some people enjoyed the fruit, while others dread them. Still others had no expression.

Some will find the fruit fantastic, some will not enjoy it. Not everybody likes durians.

I asked, "Do we have durians in Seattle ?"

The answer was, "Durians are the products of South East Asia, they are seldom seen in the States. Since durians from Thailand are exported, we can find a brand called "golden pillow" from Thailand in China Town. The taste of frozen durians definitely cannot match that of the fresh ones. We are lucky to be able to find durians in Seattle."

"What are the taboos in eating durians ?" I asked.

"The fruit must not be taken with hard liquor. After eating the durians, if we take hard liquor again, our stomach might not be able to take it. Many people died of such mixture. For our own safety, we must not drink hard liquor and eat durians at the same time."

I asked, "How many types of durians are there ?"

"There are many types of durians. Malaysia produces fragrant durians. Whereas durians from

Thailand may be sweet, dry, wet. The grade may range from excellent, good, normal to low. Durians of excellent grade are expensive and are meant for the consumption of the sultan. There are many species of low grade durians, unless you are an expert, it is difficult to distinguish them."

"I heard durians can be used as tonics."

"Yes, indeed. It is warm and heaty."

After returning to Seattle, I went to China town to buy "golden pillow" brand of durians. The durian tasted like ice cream. Although it is full of fibre, it still smells good. Fuo Qing and Fuo Qi frowned at the smell and they hid inside their rooms. They even found some clothes to pluck the door gaps.

(After returning to the States, Guru Lian Xiang wrote an article "The seductive fragrance of durians" to express her feeling. The article is appendix to this article.)

The seductive fragrance of durians by Guru Lian Xiang.

Durian is known to be the king of all fruits; and mangosteen, the queen.

By nature durian is of fire quality; and mangosteen is of water quality. Durian is a nourishing food, but it is heaty. Mangosteen is taken to cool down our bodies. Using one to counter another, the same logic as where there is action, there must be reaction.

I remembered five years ago, someone gave a box of frozen durians to us. She told me, " "golden pillow" is the best brand of durians from Thailand, you will like it. But some people might not get used to the odour. If you like it after eating, just let me know, I know where to buy them."

When I opened the box later on, there was a foul smell as stink as manure and wind from bowels. The odour was really aggressive. I fancied how come the fruit can be so stink. To me the king of all fruits is also the most smelly fruits.

I did not care how nourishing it can be, I just thought of throwing them away. But it's costly, It would be a pity to throw them away. So I decided to pinch my nose and tried the durian. At least, I could tell others I have tried durian before.

My body turned numb when the first piece of durian filled my mouth. I felt like my head was splashed with manure. Quickly I wrapped up the remaining durians and rushed out to throw them away. In fact, I vomited near the rubbish bin. Thanks but no thanks. After the event, I had to use almost a whole toothpaste to brush my teeth again and again just to clear the odour from my mouth. I was wondering how people can enjoy durian so much, do they like the durian's odour ? The horrible smell discouraged me to recollect what happened.

Between December 20, 1992 and January 10, 1993 when we were on propagation tour in Malaysia, many a time, a disciple offered the best local durians to grand master. Showing his compassion by following the crowds, although he was not very keen to eat the fruit, grand master opened the durian there and then and ate them just to make his disciple happy. He even commented that the smell was bearable. The innocent praise led to daily offering by different disciples, and grand master had to eat them again and again.

The first time he ate, he was reluctant. The second time, so, so. The third, it was OK. The fourth, not bad. He really enjoyed the nice taste of durian then.

Grand master asked me why I did not try durian, the king of all fruits. Viewing it as a drop of water in the desert, a fruit given to a starved person, and those Africans died of hunger.... I felt like eating after his persuasion.

I learned to enjoy eating durians. Thinking how fragrant, delicious, nourishing and emotional the fruit can be, I changed my attitude, my hands and cheeks frequently had durian flesh, I was happy eating them everyday.

Thinking of Malaysia now, I am reminded of durians, and the warm friendship of True Buddha disciples there.

From eating durians, I came to understand the meaning of "rejoicing in the welfare of others for a moment", as long as we can practise it in our daily life, the world will be even more perfect. If we go one step further by rejoicing in the welfare of others all the while, then we will be able to achieve more in our cultivation - just by a single thought.

Lian Hua Lin Na's tumour

In the book "The great response of Tantrayana ", I mentioned about my sick disciples after receiving empowerment from me:

Cancer cells disappeared,
Tumour subsided,
Gall stone dissolved,
Genital water evaporated,
Skin disease cured,
The blind began to see,
The deaf started to hear,
....

These are true stories. I have been slandered for more than two decades, and yet the number of my disciples multiplies tremendously. This is because they have true spiritual response and they have great confidence in me, therefore they take refuge in me. (more than 1.5 million disciples now.) As the fact cannot be denied, I am the least worried about defamation, no matter how big it is.

Some dharma masters attacked me and defamed me but once they themselves or their love ones had terminal sickness which doctors could not cure, they will remember me, and come to beg me to save them.

When the sickness is critical or fatal, they will forget about face saving. This is the moment I put my "Buddha power" to use. They will have to seek my help, as nobody else can help them.

When I was in Sibu, the newspaper reported:

"The effectiveness of his talisman is extraordinary, A young girl's tumour subsides The big burden in her heart has been released, And she stopped crying and rejoices her health."

Lian Hua Lin Na is 18 years old. Her mother, Lian Hua Liang Yi is a member of True Buddha School, Miao Li chapter in Sibu. After suffering from an infection in her right neck near her throat two years ago, a tumour as big as a chicken egg developed. After a detailed check up and biopsy, an operation was carried out in August 1991 to cut away the tumour. But not long later, the tumour grew again at the same spot, the size as big as the old one.

Lian Hua Lin Na wrote to True Buddha Sacred Garden in October 1992, asking Grand master to help her. Soon she received a reply with two talismans. Using the talismans in the prescribed way, she sincerely prayed to Grand master, Buddha and Bodhisattva for empowerment to cure her tumour.

One week later, when she touched her neck, she was delighted to find the tumour had subsided without any trace.

Lian Hua Lin Na became a living witness for Grand master on New Year day. And she also begged Grand master to empower her to ensure the tumour does not relapse.

Another disciple by the name of Chuang Miao Chun, dharma name Lian Hua Miao Chun, aged 58, lives in Bandung, Indonesia.

He suddenly felt unwell in December 1992. A check-up in a Bandung hospital on December 17 confirmed that he had stomach cancer. He will die if no operation is carried out immediately.

Knowing that her brother-in-law has cancer, Lian Hua Chai Lian, the head of Wan Sheng Chapter, Bandung, Indonesia, was shocked and sad. Together with few family members, she prayed to Grand Master, Buddha and Bodhisattva, asking a miracle to occur-- that the cancer of her brother-in-law be cured.

On 18th December, Lian Hua Chai Lian, Lian Hua Miao Chun and other family members flew to Singapore. He asked for personal empowerment by Living Buddha, before heading for Elizabeth hospital for pre-operation check-up.

When the Singapore True Buddha School's ritual for calamity eradication, merit accumulation, and souls deliverance took place at 2:00 p.m. on 19th December, Miao Chun who was supposed to be in the hospital, surprised everybody by lining up with the crowds to receive empowerment from the Living Buddha.

Lian Hua Chai Lian broke the news that a miracle happened that morning at 11:30 a.m. The doctor could not find any cancerous cells in the patient.

Chuang Miao Chun himself was a willing witness in the ritual. He asked people to take refuge in Living Buddha Lian Sheng, and cultivate True Buddha Tantra, and not to miss the salvation by Living Buddha Lian Sheng.

Cancer cured, Tumour subsided.

Other dharma masters were stunned. They sighed: "Lu Sheng-Yen is really somebody. We respect him from the bottom of our heart. But we do not like him at all, as his name overwhelms ours. Our disciples deserted us to join him. As a smart person, he should know why we, dharma masters do not like him. For the simple reason, he is too popular!"

● **Appendix**

Reports by Malaysia Daily

Malaysia Daily reported on January 3rd, 1993:

When State Deputy Industrial Development Minister Mr Shen Qiu Hui officiated the ritual, he said : "It is a golden opportunity for disciples of True Buddha School in Sawarak to see the founder Master Lu Sheng-Yen in person, to receive his empowerment and; to listen to his sermon for those who are attending the Amitabha Buddha's ritual of calamity eradication, merit accumulation and souls deliverance organised by Miao Li Chapter, Sibu."

"On one hand, these participants, by means of prayer, can eradicate calamity and accumulate merit; on the other hand, they can gain more confidence through the teaching of Grand Master to bring benefits to the country and society at large by promoting compassionate and harmonious way of life. "

The ritual organised by True Buddha School Miao Li Chapter, Sibu was held at the stadium of Catholic High School. The earth- shaking event presided by the founder of True Buddha School, Living Buddha Lian Sheng, Master Lu Sheng-Yen was a great success.

Chairman of Miao Li Chapter, the organiser,

said: " Although the population of Sibu is only slightly more than one hundred thousands, there were five thousand people participated in the ritual and more than six hundred people took refuge. Never before in Borneo's history saw such a grand ritual, not even the activities carried out by Christian or Catholicism fraternity. It's really inconceivable !"

"To propagate the True Buddha Tantra and cater for future development, Living Buddha Lian Sheng has pointed out an auspicious site for the construction of Lei Zhang Temple in Sibu !"

Living Buddha Lian Sheng arrived at Sibu at 4:30 p.m. on December 30th. He was welcomed by more than one thousand well-wishers., reporters and Lion dance troupe. Later a dinner was held to honour him.

The problems of those critically ill were solved by him in the morning of December 31. A press conference was held at the Golden Earth Hotel in the afternoon. And a sermon to one thousand two hundred disciples was given in the evening at Long Fen, Huang Clan Association.

Even on New Year Day, he did not take a rest. He held consultation session in the morning, attended a dinner given to him by the disciples at Community Hall, Sibu in the evening. Among the guests of honour were: Mr Jiang Xian Han,

Chairman City council, Sibu, Dato Chen Ren Hua, Chairman Hua Yuan group / Chinese Chamber of Commerce, Mr Xu Zhong Xiang, legal advisor to Miao Li Chapter and representatives from other Buddhism organisations.

The programmes for the evening were quite entertaining. Altogether 22 items were performed, including solo, choir, traditional dances. The performance by a ten years old girl Xu Fong Qian was well received.

January 2nd, at 11:00 a.m. Living Buddha met all the chapter heads and representatives from East Malaysia (Sarawak), Brunei, and Indonesia (Borneo) to listen to their progress reports and future plans.

6:30 p.m. Living Buddha personally presided the Amitabha Buddha's calamity eradication, merit accumulation and souls deliverance ritual.

January 3rd, he searched for a good site for the construction of Lei Zhang Temple, Sibu in the morning. And attended a lunch. In the evening, he gave a sermon at Miao Li Chapter, at the same time initiated the images and empowered the sacred shrine.

January 4th, he flew to Api and Tawau, continuing the journey to the last two destinations of his propagation tour.

Talking about four-fold stage of mindfulness in Sibu

At 6:30 p.m. on January 2nd, 1993, I gave a sermon on the four- fold stage of mindfulness in Sibu, a town beside Terang River. Sibu has slightly more than one hundred thousand inhabitants, its town centre appears to be prosperous, tranquil and peaceful.

The ritual was held at Catholic High School. Five thousand participants jammed the whole hall, with people overflowing outside. Even the school field was full, as close-circuited TV was set up for the function. Nothing like this happened before.

The four-fold stage of mindfulness is also known as the four-fold stage of thought or meditation. Most Hinayana practitioners will cultivate this dharma after they have mastered the five-fold procedure for quieting the mind.

The five-fold procedure are:
1. Vileness of all things
2. Pity for all
3. Causality
4. Right discrimination

5. Breathing

The four-fold stage of mindfulness consists of contemplating:
1. The body as impure and utterly filthy
2. Sensation or consciousness, as always resulting in suffering
3. Mind as impermanent, merely one sensation after another
4. Things in general as being dependent and without a nature of their own.
   Wisdom is derived from following the four-fold stage of mindfulness.

The four regulators to cause the mind to be in tranquillity, I mentioned in Sibu are:
1. Cutting off method- Once the thought is formed, it will be cut off immediately.
2. Free flowing method- Once the thought is formed, one must be calm and let it develop freely.
3. Watching picture method- Behave like a child, watch the pictures and not be perturbed.
4. The combination use of the last three methods.

I firmly believe, cultivating Tantra by meditation is nothing more than self-control, self-purification and self-salvation. For instance, observing precepts is a self-control measure. Meditation is indulging in self-purification, and obtaining wisdom is considered a self-salvation.

From the stand point of noble eight-fold path, self-control can be achieved by correct speech, correct livelihood, and correct conduct. Self-purification is a result of correct remembrance and correct meditation, while self-salvation is obtained by correct views, correct thought and purpose and correct zeal.

Then I gave a sermon on "Wu Shi" at Miao Li Chapter, Sibu. Wu, non, is the key to enlightenment. Wu Shi means everything is non existent. A monk from Zhao province ever said the following, "To learn Zen Buddhism, one must comprehend the meaning of "Grandmaster's barrier" thoroughly. To be enlightened as a Buddha, one must be absolute. Without these two conditions, one will only be learning from the spirit of trees. But what is Grandmaster's barrier, it is non-existence. It is the essence of Zen School, which is also known as a school of "Non".

"Believing everything is non-existent, one will be able to extricate oneself from a predicament". I concede this doctrine is the most inconceivable. It is precisely how an enlightened person feels. This is the supreme mystic enlightenment, it is almost equivalent to Nirvana itself.

To me, everything is non-existent, no matter what happened. Non- existence is the truth, the nirvana. There is no non-birth, no non-destruction.

To tell the truth, if a cultivator is not bothered by "non- birth", and "non-destruction", and is able to be in tranquillity, he has attained the fundamental law of immortality.

A treatise of Prajna mentioned, "Believe in immortality, and know the nature of non-birth and non-destruction, one will be able to flow freely, and overcome all the hindrance. That is why the law is called the wisdom of non-birth."

It also mentioned, "Wu Sheng Ren" -the wisdom of non-birth, i.e. simply put is an understanding that there is non-birth for anything big or small. He who comprehends this doctrine will not create any more karma, and will become a Bodhisattva who in his progress towards Buddhahood, will never retrograde to a lower state than to which he has attained, a Bodhisattva known as Aparivartya.

The whimper of Terang River

When in Sibu, I drew the curtains and looked at the Terang River everyday.. The murmuring water was rather yellowish. One night we took a walk at the riverside. The silent night with the silver moonlight was only broken by the murmuring sound of the flowing water.

Accompanied by the flowing sound, I walked quite a long distance. Suddenly I heard the whimper of Terang River.

Following the open confrontation between dharma masters Ji Cheng and Shu Yi, the whole Buddhism fraternity in Malaysia had been thrown into disarray. The atmosphere was both secretive and surreptitious. As the conflicts deepened, all the newspapers and magazines rushed to report the news. Are there many more untold stories ?

What is Dharma master Ji Cheng trying to cover ?

What is Dharma master Shu Yi fighting for ?

Seeing the war waged between them, the Buddhists at large are of the opinion that the pure and flawless dharma as espoused by Sakyamuni Buddha have been tainted by his ungrateful disciples. All the lay Buddhists do sincerely follow the teachings of Buddha. Just to find one of the triple gems, the monks are not embarrassed by fighting in public. The disgraceful act had made many Buddhists cold-footed and ashamed. I can't help sighing. Terang River is sobbing melancholy.

I am told Dharma Master Ji Cheng craves for fame and wealth. So is Dharma Master Shu Yi. A newspaper even reported that "They fought more than these two items." Neither have I met Dharma Master Ji Cheng, Nor have I met Dharma Master Shu Yi. But I heard the whimper of Terang River. It is full of sorrowful sarcasm.

In fact, the conflicts between these two monks, not only made Sakyamuni Buddha feel shameful, the Buddhists will also lose their beacon. They will not be happy as they do not know who is right and who is wrong, seeing them fighting for the leadership. They do not know whom to seek guidance. They are blocked instead of saved.

When there are in-fightings amongst the monks, everybody weeps. Everybody will revere if the monks can cooperate.

Which is the monk that is belligerent ? The one that holds the highest position. You know there are bound to have people who like to hold high position, so that they can look aloof and lofty. They are sacrosanct and not to be offended.

But Dharma Master Shu Yi chose to jerk him who has many infamous activities.

Although Dharma Master Ji Cheng still looked composed outwardly, he felt the pain from his heart. Because of tension, his muscle shivered. His veins were blocked, and he was groaning. He was about to die after being shot at a close distance. As a person who has high status, he had to make many speeches. But his voice is close to crying. He withered, because Dharma Master Shu Yi took another shot at him.

A quiet night with silver moonlights. The discerning Buddhists have good eye-sight. They can see that Buddhism in Malaysia is now saturated with pestilential atmosphere, the environment is as filthy as the water of Terang River.

Every part of Dharma Master Ji Cheng's body is under close scrutiny. He was too emotional, and he can't explain his compulsion. He felt upset with everything; he wanted to bite everybody. He was agitated and responded to every move. Not a behaviour from a cool and steady practitioner. All the Buddhists in Malaysia recognise this, and they could not wait any longer.

Those with experience know that it was time to leave the body that condoned fighting monks, and not to wait for the eternal darkness to dawn. (The darkness created by the monks) They know they must take refuge in True Buddha School of Buddhism, that is bright and splendid. And they must cultivate the True Buddha Tantra. They must also discard an organisation that is unhealthy, unusual, wealth-seeking, power crazy and barking at everybody.

I come to know the reasons why Buddhists of Malaysia have a liking for the True Buddha School now. They take refuge in me, participate in my ritual, and cultivate True Buddha Tantra. This is one of the reasons why suddenly there was a full house and a commotion ---monks were fighting among themselves.

Dharma Master Shu Yi was seen pulling Dharma Master Ji Cheng's ponytail again!

Vegetarian or Non-Vegetarian

I flew from Sibu to Api on January 4th, 1993. True
Buddha School has two chapters in Api, namely Ben
Jue Chapter and Lei Zhang Temple-Sabah. The
sermons I gave at the former was "Dreams" and the
latter "Vegetarian or Non-Vegetarian."

This was my second visit to Api. The first time I
came passing through Brunei in 1985. Mount
Kinabalu is the highest in South East Asia. Excerpts
of the sermon given at Ben Jue Chapter are as
follows:

Dreams are regarded by tantricas as activities
carried out by spirits when they reside in the
intermediate existence between death and
reincarnation. It is said in Tantrayana, "Immediately
after a person dies, he will have a dream-like
experience. It is unreal; but nevertheless is
sensational." That is why dreams are cultivated by
Tantricas.

We must know when we are dreaming, so that
we are alert and have self-control, and be able to
observe all the precepts. It will be even better if we
can do cultivation in our dreams.

We must also be able to control our dreams. It is
very important for us to lead the dreams, because

while we are dreaming we may have all the six mystic powers as follows:

1. Control the flight to anywhere we want.
2. Control the deva-vision.
3. Ability to hear any sound anywhere.
4. Knowing the thought of all other minds.
5. Knowledge of former existences of self and others.
6. To have the consciousness of the waning of vicious propensities.

Dreams may be good or bad. Good dreams are encouragement given by Buddha and Bodhisattva. Bad dreams are a reflection of our unwholesome karma.

We must put in even more effort when we have good dreams. On the other hand, when we always have bad dreams we must do repentance ritual, do prostration, make offerings to Buddha, give alms and refrain from doing bad deeds. A tantrica must carry out fire Puja to turn bad dreams into good ones.

Milarepa, the grand master of Nyingmapa is known to have two prominent dreams.

1. He was told by the space-travelling goddess in a dream to obtain the Gangis Mudra that will enable a person to gain enlightenment instantly. After he woke up, he related the dream to his

teacher, who immediately set out to India to learn the dharma from Grand master Naropa.

2. He dreamed that his mother had passed away, and their garden was not cultivated for a long time. He bade farewell to his teacher and returned home. True enough, his mother passed away many years ago, and their garden laid wasted.

Tantricas believe in dream-cultivating. It is a cultivation of intermediate existence between death and reincarnation.

The excerpt of my sermon at Lei Zhang Temple-Sabah is as follows:

Eating vegetarian and non-vegetarian meals were mentioned in Agama Sutra. In fact, Brahmajala Sutra and Surangama Sutra explained the controversy in detail. It's a pity that Buddhism scholar Lu Chen had concluded that these two Sutras may be a forgery.

During Sakyamuni's era, monks did not cook their own meal. They went out with their alms and asked for food. They ate whatever alms they can get. (It is a fact.)

Sakyamuni Buddha received his last alm from a blacksmith by the name of Chunda. After eating some contaminated meat, he knew that he was about to leave the samsara world, and accordingly he went into Nirvana at the grove of Sal (teak) trees near Kusinagara city.

I must stress the fact that Sakyamuni Buddha did not insist that all of us must be vegetarian. And Buddhism is also not a religion that advocates all must be vegetarian. It was the rebellious disciple of Buddha Devadatta who championed the statement of five means i.e.

1. Wear only monk's garments
2. Eat only once a day
3. Eat only vegetarian food
4. Not to be served
5. Stay in straw hut

Sakyamuni Buddha always adapted to the wishes of others. He himself ate fish.

Devadatta used the ascetic practice to win the hearts of others. It was Devadatta, the rebellious disciple, who became the first proponent of vegetarian meal.

I surmise, "souls deliverance and offering rituals are more important than vegetarian meal". A verse from Sakyamuni Buddha explained it all:

Eighty Four thousand beings (bacteria), found in a mouthful of clean water, If we do not chant the Mantra, It will be like killing other sentient beings.

A poem descended by Living Buddha Ji Gong

I flew from Api to Tawau on January 5th,1993. Tawau is a remote small town in Malaysia. The population is small and the streets are narrow.

But to my surprise, Tawau boasts one of the most beautiful and solemn Lei Zhang Temple. I named it Lian Hu (Lotus Pond) Lei Zhang Temple.

Buddhism thrives in Tawau. There are Malaysia Tawau Buddhist Association, Lian Hai Fuo Xue Hui, Fuo Guang Si, Puo Zhao Si and the new addition, Lian Hu Lei Zhang Si.

The population of the town though small is very complicated. There are Chinese, Malays, Aborigines, Filipinos, and Indonesians. Many Filipinos came to Tawau illegally, as a result the usually calm and tranquil Tawau now faces quite a bit of security problem (Smuggling of liquor and tobacco). The demarcating lines of residential areas for different races are very distinctive.

Although the streets are not very clean, there are many eating stalls. It is very busy at night. There are China Town and Malay Town in the city. From the town centre, one can go to any place within five minutes' drive. Few tourists are found in town.

I spotted a mosque in town centre. The religions and customs are quite different. The buildings concentrate on the three main streets. In my view, the Macro Polo Hotel that I stayed is the biggest building.

Although there are many shops, row upon row on the not so elegant street, the buildings are old and dilapidated. Moreover the weather is hot and there is nothing that interest me.

There are few houses in the sub-urban, the roads are wide and the air more refreshing.

I do not understand why it is called Tawau (Small lake). Small may seem right, but there is no lake at all. I only saw a sea. They pointed at one side of the sea and told me that is Indonesia; then another direction and said Philippines is over there. May be other races become greedy because of its proximity.

Sunlight reflected in the mighty waves. It is difficult to detect where the sea ends and the sky begins. The sky and the water are of the same colour.

Facing the sea and leaning against a hill, Tawau is quite flat. Its sub-urban is rich in greenery. The hill that I went up, had a picturesque scenery. On seeing this, a visitor will feel peaceful and forget about his worries.

Before my arrival in Tawau, a commotion was already created. The local newspaper, Morning News reported:

Vajra Guru Lu Sheng-Yen arrives today, He makes fairy tales and miracles.

Even Living Buddha Ji Gong joined in to advise his believers to treasure the opportunity.

Living Buddha Lian Sheng, Vajra Guru Lu Sheng-Yen, the highest achiever in Tantra cultivation showed many miracles and created fairly tales.

The man of the moment in Buddhism fraternity who is well known for his mystic powers will fly in from Api to Tawau this afternoon at 2:00 p.m. Before his arrival, he already showed another miracle. The grand master of Purple Hour Pavilion, De Jiao Hui, Tawau, i.e. Living Buddha Ji Gong descended a written decree through a medium on 24th and 31st last month on the subject of the imminent propagation tour of Living Buddha Lian Sheng to Tawau. The poem is as follows:

Lian Sheng the saint travels the four sea,

painstakingly he entices people to cultivate,

his child-like speech is innocent and attracts attention,

be respectful to your relatives and pray to Buddha,
we must establish causality when it is due,
if our unwholesome karma is too many,
we shall miss the opportunity,
It will be difficult for us to meet him again this life.
Don't listen to rumour and distance him.
17th is an auspicious date for merit accumulation,
A ritual will be conducted by a renown saint in
this world,
all of you must have a relation with him.
The souls deliverance will lead to calamity
eradication.

In his written decree, Living Buddha Ji Gong instructed in advance that all his believers must treasure this once a life time magnificent opportunity, to listen to Living Buddha's sermon, to learn dharma from him, to take refuge in him, to receive empowerment from him, and to attend his ritual for merit accumulation, calamity eradication and souls deliverance.

It is evident that all the Buddhas, Bodhisattvas and devas are happy with the arrival of Living Buddha Lian Sheng. And they are protecting and supporting True Buddha School of Buddhism.

We are given the understanding that when Living Buddha Lian Sheng last came in 1985, many of those who listened to his sermon, and received his empowerment had earlier on dreamed that Avalokitesvara Bodhisattva told them a Vajra Guru will come to teach the True dharma. As True Buddha Tantra is hard to come by, everybody should go and listen to his sermon and receive empowerment from him.

Living Buddha Lian Sheng is reputed to be one of the few practitioners who can really invoke Buddha, Bodhisattva, and Dharma Protector to descend and help people.

The following gurus will be accompanying him to Tawau on this tour :

Lian Xiang, Lian Man, Chang Zhi, Chang Ren (all from USA), Lian Zhi (Canada), Lian Shi, Lian Ting (Taiwan) and Lian Xuan (Singapore).

Living Buddha will conduct a Padmakumara Merit accumulation, calamity eradication and souls deliverance ritual on 9th evening at the Ba Zhong Qiu Fu Memorial Hall. He will use his mystic powers to display "soul deliverance" and "merit accumulation" Mudra to invoke the descendance of cosmic energy so that: the participants will avoid calamity, recover from sickness,accumulate merit, prolong their lives, and have good fortune.

He will also repent on behalf of the wondering souls, debtors, so that all previous hatred can be forgiven and forgotten. The souls of those deceased can be uplifted and be feted by Buddha to the Western Pure Land.

For the last two weeks, Living Buddha Lian Sheng conducted many rituals in Singapore, Kuala Lumpur, and Sibu. Tens of thousands of people attended them. It is a commotion in Buddhism.

We were told when Living Buddha conducted a ritual in Hong Kong on December 28th, 1991, more than one million people registered themselves. This can be considered an all time record in Buddhism history. Living Buddha Lian Sheng made a great vow to break his bones and sacrifice his life for the salvation of all sentient beings. He used the dharma powers from Buddhism and Taoism to transfer all the unwholesome karma of others to himself, he suffered all kinds of sickness on behalf of others. After a torture of three days and three nights, he saved many of his disciples who were suffering from all kinds of terminal illness.

When the ritual was in progress that night, three rays of colourful rainbows suddenly appeared in the dark sky. A miracle that was unseen, unheard of.

Some said that this was proof that Living Buddha Lian Sheng had already attained a level that he could change his body into a rainbow at will.

Living Buddha will be staying in Tawau for five days. Apart from conducting ritual to be held on 9th 7:30 p.m. at Ba Zhong Qiu Fu Memorial Hall, he will also be giving an important sermon on 7th 7:30 p.m. at the concourse of Lian Hu Lei Zhang Temple. At the same time, he will empower those newly joining the School.

Those who take refuge and receive empowerment, will have Buddha power after Living Buddha uses mystic power to energize them. Those disciples who received his empowerment will also be able to have an empowered body. By virtue of Living Buddha's power derived from cultivation, all the disciples will be enlightened as a Buddha. His empowerment is known : to cure sickness, to remove worries, to eradicate calamity, to settle court case, to accumulate merit for the participants, to prolong life, to gain benefit, to result in good interpersonal relationship with others , to have more children, to have loving kindness, and to respect others.

It is also said those who have taken refuge in him will be protected by 36 numbers of good gods and more.

Those wishing to take part in the above-mentioned ritual or taking refuge in Living Buddha Lian Sheng may register themselves at the Lian Hu Lei Zhang Temple.

For the convenience of those wishing to take refuge in Living Buddha Lian Sheng, Master Lu Sheng-Yen, we write below the procedure:

Those wishing to take refuge in Living Buddha Lian Sheng and obtain his lineage in True Buddha School can use one of the two methods.

Taking refuge personally-make prior appointment for the date and time and fly to Seattle-Redmond's True Buddha Tantric Garden to receive personal empowerment by Living Buddha.

After the ceremony, Living Buddha will give out the acknowledgement certificate, his photograph and cultivation text to the newly initiated so that they can obtain the lineage.

Taking refuge by letter-Because disciples could be from all over the world, it is not possible for all to take refuge personally. Those wishing to take refuge may face the direction of the rising sun on either 1st or 15th day of lunar month and recite the Mantra of taking refuge three times.

"Namo guru peh, Namo Buddha Ya, Namo dharma Ya, Namo sanggha Ya, with the guidance of

Lian Sheng the saint, I now take refuge in True Buddha."

After chanting three times, do prostration three times. (either on the 1st or 15th day of Lunar month)

Living Buddha on his part will hold a remote empowerment session at the True Buddha Tantric Garden on those days to empower those who are unable to take refuge in person.

Those who have completed the rites at home must then write a letter giving the details of their real name, address, age, and any amount of offering to True Buddha Tantric Garden, highlighting "Taking refuge and empowerment" at the envelope. After receiving the letter, Lian Sheng the saint will post the acknowledgement certificate, his photograph and tell the disciple what dharma to cultivate first. This is how the lineage is obtained.

The address of True Buddha Tantric Garden is
Sheng-Yen Lu
17102 NE 40th CT.
Redmond WA. 98052
U.S.A.

Images in the sky

A disciple by the name Lian Hua Di Jing brought his father Lian Hua Ming Xiong, his mother Lian Hua Chai Xiang, and his younger brother Lian Hua Di Lin to Tawau to take part in the True Buddha ritual. They sat in the car for more than ten hours from 7:00 o' clock in the morning to 7:00 o'clock in the evening.

Lian Hua Di Jin wrote a letter to me later and enclosed some photographs for me. He described the story of "images in the sky" in detail.

" After the ritual, I followed grand master's instruction and took a look at the sky. Some of them said the stars seemed strange while others said it was the moon. My brother and I insisted that it must be the moon, because it was so glittering, clear, and serene. Before the rainbows were formed, we took a picture of the moon. When we were asked whether there was anything in the moon, I replied that I was not sure. But the moon was beautiful indeed.

Not long later, an inconceivable phenomena appeared, the moon radiated rounds and rounds of lights. We placed our camera in the tripod. The speed of the camera was set to one second, and the

158

aperture enlarged before we took the shot. At that time, most of the people had already left for home. My brother, my mother and I were still looking at the moon ! (enclosed are two photographs) One of the photographs looks like the heart Mantra wheel of Grand Master. In view of this, We printed more copies for our friends. We hope they will believe Grand Master is really an enlightened Living Buddha who can change his body into rainbow lights. I am delighted all of them have more confidence now.

The above was the letter from Lian Hua Di Jin.

Rainbow is both real and unreal. Life is a dream and an illusion. As passer-by, why don't we pluck the rainbow and get rid of all the suffering in life.

The story of "Images in the sky" is both magnificent and unique.

When Jesus Christ was born, a big star radiated at him.

When Buddha was born, nine dragons bathed him with water. And the earth had six earthquakes.

When I presides over rituals, there are many different images in the sky....

Someone saw my body changing into rainbow.

Someone saw me sitting in the moon.

Someone saw my heart Mantra appearing in the

moon.

Layers of rainbows surrounded the moon.

Someone saw a lot of flowers dripping from the sky, red, yellow, white, purple....

The newspaper reported that:

A record was set for the ritual by Buddhism organisation in our state. Many people experienced spiritual response in the perfect and magnificent ritual.

The Padmakumara ritual for merit accumulation, calamity eradication, and souls deliverance organised by True Buddha School Lian Hu Lei Zhang Temple Tawau has broken a record to be the most successful ritual held by any religious organisation in the state.

The chairman of Lian Hu Lei Zhang Temple said the ritual was presided by Living Buddha Lian Sheng. More than twenty thousand registered for the ritual and more than three thousand Buddhists and well-wishers turned up personally. Qiu Fu Memorial Hall was full to the beam. This was the second time True Buddha School held the ritual in Tawau. More than one thousand foreigners came to take part. It was news in Tawau. The feat is even admired by other religious organisations.

Apart from Buddhists who came to see the charm of Living Buddha Lian Sheng, and took part in the ritual, many prominent people , politicians and members of other religious bodies from the state also rushed to the opening ceremony and ritual. They paid respect to the accomplishment of Living Buddha Lian Sheng.

The ritual was perfect and magnificent. Many people experienced spiritual response. Half way through the ritual many disciples standing outside the hall started to scream continuously when they looked at the sky. Many more inside the memorial hall ran out and did the same. They saw seven rays of five-coloured rainbows appearing gradually in the surrounding of the moon. Some lucky ones even reported that they saw the solemn looking image of Living Buddha Lian Sheng in the moon.

People from other districts of Tawau also reported they saw the same spectacular scene. Nobody heard of the moon surrounded by rainbow at night before. This was a miracle.

We were given to understand Living Buddha and rainbow have deep relationship. Whenever and wherever he presides a ritual, rainbow lights will always surface. According to Tantrayana belief, this is a clear evidence that Living Buddha Lian Sheng has achieved the level of "changing his body into rainbow lights."

When Living Buddha was officiating at the opening and initiating ceremony in the morning of 8th, a big white lotus was seen in the sky. Living Buddha Lian Sheng is the reincarnation of white Lotus Lad from the Western Pure Land.

Yang Jun He said, Living Buddha Lian Sheng is the most compassionate person in the Buddhism world. He is well known to have brought salvation to many. Before coming to Tawau, Grandmaster has visited Singapore, Johor, Kuala Lumpur and Sibu. He will have to rush to Hong Kong tomorrow to conduct another ritual and succour more human beings in suffering.

While in Tawau, Grand master worked from dawn to mid-night to serve his believers. He held consultation sessions, paid visits to other religious bodies, officiated the opening ceremony of Lian Hu Lei Zhang Temple, gave dharma talk, empowered his disciples, and conducted ritual.

It is very tiring for the Grand master. In view of his vow and great compassion, he was able to succour more than five hundred new disciples at the ritual in Tawau. Lei Zhang Si has close to one thousand members now. Members of the temple wish to thank the Grand master for his presence and great cause.

On behalf of the temple he also liked to invite those who had just taken refuge in Living Buddha to attend the weekly group cultivation session, cultivating the superb and valuable True Buddha Tantra together.

The success of the ritual was mainly attributed to helps rendered by dharma brothers and sisters from local and overseas. Mr Yang would like to take this opportunity to thank all of them whole- heartedly.

Question and Answer session with reporters in Tawau

Date : January 6th, 1993

Venue : Lian Hu-Lei Zhang Temple (Auspicious Hall)

Participants : Living Buddha and reporters from various newspapers.

Q. Can you please tell us, Living Buddha, how do you become a controversial figure?

A. Ever since I started to walk the path two decades ago, I have been termed a controversial character. My saga is almost a fairly tale. I was brought to Western Pure Land, Maha Double Lotus Pond. This adventure is always contentious.

Q. Are you the Pope of True Buddha School ?

A. No, I am not. I considered myself the founder. A person who propagates dharma.

Q. What is the meaning of Living Buddha?

A. Buddha is an enlightened person. A Living Buddha is one who knows the pristine nature of mind and have it appeared in himself. He is able to control his own life and death.

Q. Youth Group of Malaysian Buddhism Association

made a statement that Malaysia is a country free of natural disaster and man-made calamity, why must True Buddha School hold a ritual for calamity eradication, and merit accumulation ?

A. True Buddha School has been holding such rituals all over the world, not only in Malaysia. You say there is no natural disaster in Malaysia ? What about the flood after a heavy down-pour ? Political upheaval ? How can you say there are no natural disaster and man-made calamity in Malaysia? The youth group is very narrow-minded and full of jealousy. They indulge in parochialism, we should be not bothered.

Q. Dharma Master Xing Yun came to do propagation also, why was he not criticized ?

A. When Dharma Master Xing Yun came, Newspapers accused him of indulging in banditry, and warned the follow Buddhists not to fall into his trap. They censured him "occupying a mountain in order to be the leader of Buddhist world." Newspapers and Magazine reprimanded him vehemently. Even I sympathize him. It is not true to say he was not criticized at all. (The reporter concerned was rendered speechless.)

Q. In your opinion, is this the right behaviour ?

A. We must learn to praise one another. Attacking one another is not a good solution. Buddhism will thrive if one monk starts to praise another. At this juncture, Islam as a religion is the biggest in the whole world, and Buddhism is the smallest. Buddhism does not flourish, parochialism is the main cause.

Q. What is the definition of a Buddha ?

A. A person who has gained enlightenment.

Q. You have once warned a news reporter that he should not write rubbish, otherwise he might be hit by lightning. Is this true?

A. I have been a reporter myself in Taiwan for more than ten years. The reminder on the wall behind us read:

"Find the truth, report them objectively and impartially." I was very open-minded in a press conference held in Kuala Lumpur. All the questions raised were answered. One of the reporters just wrote something I did not say. This is the type of reporters I like to censure.

Q. You are very happy when people call you "Mara ", Are you not?

A. Yes, I am very happy indeed. I consider myself an ordinary person, not somebody who has the quality to be called a "Mara". If I am really a Mara, how can those who scolded me still be alive ? You must know not only Buddha can achieve a profound state of spiritual cultivation, so can a Maha-Mara. Even the level of achievement by an ordinary Mara is inconceivable. We must not look down on them, not even that of other human beings. If I am given the title of a Mara, I am surely delighted, although my level of achievement does not qualify yet.

Q. How do you begin to learn the Tantra ?

A. Initially, it was between mid-night and one o'clock in the morning. My teacher, master "Three mountains-nine-marquees" who is transparent came to teach me. He whispered Mantra into my ear. I learned all the Mudra from him. He taught me for many years. The teaching method is true, it is the whole truth, nothing but the truth. I did not lie. But there are people who chose not to believe them, so I end up a controversial character.

Q. It is said that there are only four righteous Buddhist organisations in Tawau, namely Tawau Buddhist Association, Fuo Guang Si, Ji Shi Lin Pu Zhao Si, and Lian Hai Fuo Xue Hui. The rest are heretical Buddhism, what do you think, Living Buddha ?

A. All the religions in this world consider themselves to be one and only righteous religion, other religions are heretical beliefs. To the Christians, Buddhism is Satanism. All the Buddhist organisations are the same, they claim to be the righteous beliefs. They will never openly say they are radical. Likewise it is not possible for True Buddha School to say it is heretical. When we proclaim we are righteous, the rest will scream at us. When the achievements of different schools are compared, people will be able to reach a conclusion on which school is righteous, and which school is not.

Q. What are the achievements of True Buddha School ?

A. It is quite common for monks from True Buddha School to have Sarira in their remains after cremations. Even ninety percent of the dead convicts achieved the same feat. We have living witnesses and evidence to support our claims. These are all true. These achievements will go a long way to prove that True Buddha School is a righteous form of Buddhism.

Q. What is the future plan for True Buddha School?

168

A. We do not have any plan. I mean we let nature take its own course. Succouring more people, so that they come to comprehend the truth espoused by Buddha is our hope. We wish them cultivating True Buddha Tantra personally and be enlightened as a Buddha. As a human being, we are just a guest passing through this Samsara world, fame and wealth are nothing but dreams only. I do not wish to set up a religious kingdom in this world.

Treasure the opportunity to learn the dharma this life

Let me reproduce a piece of news by a reporter from Tawau first.

Vjara Guru Living Buddha Lian Sheng, Master Lu Sheng-Yen said "The Tantra as expounded by the True Buddha School is very suitable for the contemporary cultivation. People cultivating it will have great attainment and be enlightened as a Buddha eventually. "

He said, "True Buddha Tantra is great to be cultivated personally. It is very difficult to find such good Tantra, therefore we must treasure the opportunity to learn the dharma this life."

He also said, "Living Buddha is really a person who advocates personal cultivation. He enjoys the true dharma taste from his cultivation. He is able to show his Buddha nature. As he has attained enlightenment, he is the person who understands the whole truth of the universe."

Two nights ago, Living Buddha Lian Sheng Vajra Guru gave a talk on Tantra and presided over an empowerment ceremony held at Lian Hu Lei Zhang Temple for believers who came to have relationship, or to take refuge in him. More than two thousand people took part in the ceremony. The crowds jammed the whole temple, not even a drop of water could trickle through. Living Buddha Lian Sheng said, "Combining the dharma from Sutrayana and Tantrayana, I used an inductive method to organise the True Buddha Tantra." He believes that the Tantra is suitable for contemporary cultivation. The time taken is short - only half an hour to one hour per day. "If you spend a little time each day, strive to purify your body, speech, and mind. Once they are clean, you can start cultivating the Buddha nature. One of these days, your Buddha nature will appear, and you will be enlightened as a Buddha."

Living Buddha believes that True Buddha Tantra is the best. He himself has walked through the whole course. From four foundation, Guru Yoga, Deity Yoga, Supreme Tantra, Vajra dharma, and finally Maha-perfection. Lately he refined the cultivation stages in more details. The sequence of progress now is from four foundation, Guru Yoga, Deity Yoga, to precious vase - Qi. The last item is the beginning of inner cultivation. Followed by internal fire, opening of middle vein, and unlocking the five wheels - the five vajrasattva.

Living Buddha said he has cultivated personally

and put in a lot of effort to walk through the whole course himself. He now returned from the destination to tell us it is the right way to go in order to be enlightened as a Buddha. He stressed that he is a truly enlightened teacher. There are very few such teachers in the world, since most of them are not perfect themselves, they are unable to explain the dharma correctly.

They just used the text and said, "I read and you listen, you must trust the book, you don't have to believe in me." But Living Buddha is different, he has gone to the destination. And now he is back to teach people to walk the path, that is why he can be called a truly enlightened teacher. Those who are not sure with the dharma and still have the courage to teach are at best "unclear teacher", or " a parrot learning to speak."

It is difficult to find a truly enlightened teacher to teach dharma, therefore we must treasure when he gives a sermon on dharma and Buddhism theory. Since the teacher has comprehended the topics perfectly, his talk will lead everybody to the correct path.

Living Buddha said, "Life is impermanent, we must cultivate soon. We must look for a truly enlightened teacher, that is why we must take refuge in Living Buddha Lian Sheng. We must learn True Buddha Tantra from him. Although Tantra is easily available, it is better to cultivate True Buddha Tantra which is effective. " Can we verify what Living Buddha has just claimed ?" Sure, after cultivating the True Buddha Tantra, the dead convicts who were True Buddha disciples had sarira in their remains. These are facts not to be denied.

He also appealed to all True Buddha disciples to treasure the opportunity to learn the dharma this life. Since they have come across the Tantra, and cultivated personally. They should not give up or recede in their cultivation. They must understand the Tantra and be unified with it, eventually success will come.

Living Buddha Lian Sheng pointed out in this world there are few people who have written 103 books. He is one of them. He cultivates daily for more than 23 years, and that without any break. He is one of the few people who have done that.

On the offensive slander and rejection he faced, he sighed with emotion. He lamented that people attacked him because he founded the True Buddha School and called himself Living Buddha. When he was attacked, the school was also attacked. Those who attacked him chose to ignore the effort in cultivation he put in, and the 103 books he wrote. His success was attributed to zeal and hard work. People always chose to find faults with his success and overlooked his painstaking effort. They only complained that why people gave land, house, Rolex watch, and best car to Living Buddha. They never thought that these things were given because he put in a lot of effort in personal cultivation, they did not come from the air.

In Lian Hu Lei Zhang Temple, I planted a mangosteen tree, and guru Lian Xiang a Jambu tree.

On January 8th, 1993, at 11:00 a.m. I initiated the Lian Hu Lei Zhang Temple, among others, True Buddha hall, Goddess of golden mother hall, True Buddha Tantric garden, Ksitigarbha hall, virtue hall, fortune hall......

Persons responsible for the construction of the temple are:

Lian Hua Qun He
Lian Hua Yan Shen
Lian Hua Guo Zhong etc.

I wrote a verse to commemorate In the samsara world, ten of thousands of lotus flowers blossom, the view at the lake was brilliant like a raging fire, the drum and thunder will shock for years, honour the Buddha and find the truth.

People have questioned me how a Lei Zhang Temple can be built in a small town like Tawau. They want to know the reason. I believe by keeping close to True Buddha Tantra, we can achieve outstanding result. True Buddha Tantra is the most respectable and valuable Tantra, what are its specialities ?

They include: purification, invocation, taking refuge, prostration, making offering, recital of sutra, mudra, visualisation, chanting mantra, meditation, recital of Buddha's name, transference.

Outwardly, we cultivate the purification of body, speech and mind. Inwardly, we cultivate the pure light from Qi, Mai and Ming Dian. (vital energy, veins, and luminous point)

It consists of combined wisdom of Manjusri and Samantabhadra's ten vows. We do not rest on our laurels. True Buddha Tantra can be described as a dharma vessel, big enough to bring countless sentient beings to the other shore (enlightenment).

The attainments of Lian Hu Lei Zhang Temple is no mean feat. The spirit of the temple reflects in the structure of the whole building. The unrivalled True Buddha Tantra is very charming.

● **Appendix**

The speech by Guru Lian Xiang

Guru Lian Xiang of True Buddha School, Seattle, USA said at the initiation and opening ceremony today that during the construction of the temple, three miracles have happened. She pointed out that the cause of building the temple is remarkable. When Living Buddha last went to Singapore for propagation, Lian Hua Yan Sheng and a few disciples from Lian Hu Chapter went to Singapore and asked Living Buddha for empowerment so that the planned construction work can progress smoothly. Three miracles have since happened. First, after they returned from Singapore, the permit to build Lian Hu Lei Zhang Temple was approved immediately. Second, the building fund was a miserable ten thousand after the permit was obtained. The committee members and follow disciples nevertheless went ahead with the building plan. They asked for empowerment by Buddha and Bodhisattva. And miracle happened again. Whenever money was short, Padmakumara will show his mystic power by delivering the money. Third, when Living Buddha confirmed he will officiate the initiation and opening ceremony, only six months were left for the construction work - a time just enough for the construction of an ordinary house. As you can see, this solemn temple needs time and effort to build. During construction, follow cultivators asked for empowerment by Buddha and Bodhisattva, so that the rain came as and when required. True enough, favours were given to the True Buddha disciples. During day time when work had to be carried out, it never rained. When the cement needed water at night, it rained automatically. It is really a miracle.

The greatest contemporary Tantrica, Living Buddha Lian Sheng this morning at 9:30 a.m. officiated the initiation and opening ceremony of the True Buddha Temple - Lian Hu Lei Zhang Temple. More than one thousand people attended the function. The crowds jammed the roads leading to the temple. The grand temple, completed in under six months, is situated at True Treasure way off Xin An Road 3rd mile. The temple's surroundings are elegant. It is quiet in a noisy place. The True Buddha hall enshrined Sakyamuni Buddha, the three saints of the Western Pure Land, Avalokitesvara, Mahasthama, Padmakumara and four Isvara gods. On the right of the main hall is Ksitigarbha hall, where great vow Ksitigarbha Bodhisattva is enshrined. Virtue hall is just behind it. On the left of the main hall is goddess of golden mother hall where Jade-Pond-Golden-Mother is enshrined. These pure and solemn images were all imported from China.

Inside the temple is also a room that can accommodate more than one hundred people cultivating together. Another auditorium will be used to train True Buddha personnel. There are library, office and dinning room in the temple also.

Guru Lian Xiang opined that the solemn temple is a good place for cultivation. Follow cultivators must uphold the True Buddha spirit and view salvation and cultivation as the most urgent tasks. She said two days ago she planted a tree on the left side of the main hall. The tree can only grow properly if there are sunlight, water and tender care. To be fruitful in our cultivation, we must grow, expand and bear fruit like a growing tree.

True Buddha Lamp

True Buddha School has a chapter by the name of "Ren Shan" in Sandakan. The Chapter Head Liu Zhen Ge came along many disciples to take part in the ritual at Tawau. During the dinner held on January 7th, he sang a song entitled "True Buddha Lamp."

The lyrics are as follows:
An old lamp,
was lit in the old India,
a place called Bodhigaya.
And now another lamp,
is being lit in the west,
Seattle in the States,
Sakyamuni is dead though,
his wisdom lamp is inherited by
Living Buddha Lian Sheng, who will
succour all sentient beings,
Take refuge in True Buddha, and
cultivate True Buddha Tantra.

(After all the sentient beings are enlightened then I shall become a Buddha-that is the great vow of Living Buddha Lian Sheng. As a good teacher is hard to come by, we must whole- heartedly honour

our teacher, treasure the Tantra, and cultivate personally.

Om Guru Lian Sheng Siddhi Hum! Padmakumara Heart Mantra. Let us hope the True Buddha lamp can be passed on, and the lights radiate everywhere.)

His charming voice was impressive. His thought profound and full of confidence. The melody lingers in our mind.

The song reminded me of:

Lamp - one of the eight offerings. It is brightness, which is the ultimate aim of all Buddhists. The correct view of True Buddha School is "Brightness of emptiness."

The lamp of the poor - In the Sutra of Ajatasatru, a poor old lady used all her saving to buy a lamp and offered it to Sakyamuni. The small lamp was what she had. All the lamps went off after a strong wind, only the one offered by the old lady was still burning. Sakyamuni Buddha prophesied the old lady will be a future Buddha.

The lamp symbolises wisdom.

Bright Lamp Buddha - whose full name was Sun-Moon-Bright-Lamp Buddha was a Buddha of the past. In the present era, he is Sakyamuni Buddha. He pointed out previously that Sakyamuni Buddha would show the six signs of auspicious look and expound the Lotus Sutra.

I also think of Lighting Lamp Buddha. When he was born, the surrounding was very bright as if lamps were being lit. Accordingly he was called Lighting Lamp Prince and Lighting Lamp Buddha after his enlightenment. His previous name was Tranquil Light Buddha.

In the second Asankhya (there are four asankhya kalpas in the rise, duration, end of every universe), when Sakyamuni was still cultivating, Lighting Lamp Buddha was just born into the world. Sakyamuni Buddha bought a five petalled lotus to make offering to him. He also asked Lighting Lamp Buddha to step on the hair he buried in the mud. Lighting Lamp Buddha then prophesied that Sakyamuni will be a future Buddha with the same name.

There are people who believe that "Lu Sheng-Yen has done something he should not have done. He should not make comparison with Sakyamuni Buddha. He is really stupid."

My explanation, "A Buddhist aspires to become a Buddha. If he does not make comparison with Buddha then who else will ?" I continue, "Nowadays, Sakyamuni Buddha is enshrined at a high position. The Buddha has to be seated; but we human beings are standing. There is a wrong perception that a Buddha will be a Buddha, and human beings are human beings forever. As a Buddhist, we must learn from Buddha until our body, speech, and mind are the same as that of Sakyamuni Buddha, then we can gain the same enlightenment as Sakyamuni did."

Someone remarked, "Lu Sheng-Yen does not look like a fool, he is too smart a human being. May be what he said is right!"

Another person said, "What Lu Sheng-Yen said is marvellous, he has gained an unfair advantage, his Padmakumara photograph already has a lotus seat! "

I am now telling the truth to all of you:

Sakyamuni Buddha said it long long ago, heart, Buddha and sentient beings are one and the same. Not two or three different things. He also said it at the same time that all sentient beings are Buddhas. Human is the same as Buddha. They are of the same origin, and not two different species.

I follow the footstep of Sakyamuni Buddha closely when I learn Buddhism. Close enough for me to embrace, and embody him. Two of us are just like one single person. I am Sakyamuni, and Sakyamuni is me.

To learn Buddhism, we have to do so. Many monks in this world believe wrongly that those who are in high position must be respected and not be emulated or compared. They will not gain enlightenment. They only know the ritual of kowtow and prostration. In fact, these monks are the biggest fool on earth.

They are a herd of ass deserted by the Buddha.

Two magnificent rituals

On January 9th , 1993 the ritual held at Qiu Fu Memorial hall was magnificent. It broke a record. The complimentary terms used by the newspapers and magazines are aplenty :Full house, not even a drop of water could trickle through, a sea of people, never before, many spiritual response, breaking records, what a perfection, images in the sky, renaissance of Buddhism, rebirth of Buddha, Sakyamuni the second...

These complimentary terms have reaffirmed that Living Buddha's magic power is infinitely resourceful. There are few people like him in this world.

Then on January 13th, 1993 I went to Hong Kong's Hong Kang stadium and presided a fire puja ritual. It was another ritual attended by more than ten thousand people. There were many complimentary terms used also. Many newspapers and magazines reported the event. My picture was used as the cover. The headline was "Lu Sheng-Yen comes again!"

At the Har Par Villa, Hong Kong, two ladies were at a store.

"The dharma master you talked about is over

184

there." One of them said.

"I think it must be him."

"He is not very tall, with a perfect face, long ears, he looks like a Buddha to me."

"His real name is Lu Sheng-Yen."

"Lu Sheng-Yen, the one who can cure your sickness? "

"Yes, that is the one I mentioned." replied another lady.

Wherever you go in Hong Kong, when the term Living Buddha Lian Sheng is mentioned, people will show an astounded look. He is not only well known to the buddhists. People all over the walks, from the highest class to the lowest, including the young and old , know about him. They asked questions like

"Is he a human being ?"

"Does he look frightening ?"

"Is he an intriguing person ?"

No matter what do you think, the ritual held in Singapore, Johor Bahru, Kuala Lumpur, Penang, Sibu, Tawau, and Hong Kong clearly show that True Buddha School is up and coming. The attainments of Master Lu are extraordinary. You can feel them from his movements, and his look. His ritual-prominent, his personality- outstanding.

I talked about sarira (relics) in the rituals held in

Tawau and Hong Kong. Although the world is very big, it is rare a venerated monk has sarira in his remains. We hail the news sarira were found in the remains of those dead convicts who took refuge in True Buddha School. Alas ! those people from other religious bodies, who attacked me pull a long face immediately. As usual, they used a low tone and fabricated an unwarranted charge, "impossible!"

This time I used a simple and direct method to counter:

Human testimony - Ex-convict on dead rows who was released from prison and family members of the dead convicts concerned.

Material evidence - Sarira Exhibition.

The human testimony and material evidence had frightened them into a fainthearted turtle, without utter a word.

We smile and they cry.

True Buddha School prides itself that human beings have high attainments. It is never easy to set up a true school in Buddhism in the first place. But we are able to show the result - the cultivation fruit. True Buddha School will go on to be the main stream of Buddhism, this is an unavoidable trend.

Many venerated monks are indeed very foolish. They unduly treasure their lives. By all means they try to overwhelm Lu Sheng-Yen. this is because many of their disciples have decided to join Lu Sheng-Yen. And what they did was just making a lot of noise, since they cannot produce sarira. And at times, they foolishly pretended like a moth darting into a flame- to show their untrue bravery.

The dead convicts from True Buddha School put in unceasing effort in their cultivation, it is a tragic experience, it is a miserable beauty. The raging flame has charted the brightness of True Buddha school. The venerated monks are moth darting into a flame. They tried to control the news media, so that news about dead convicts have sarira in their remains are not divulged. They are even more stupid than we thought.

I say,

sarira are found in Sakyamuni,

sarira are found in the ten chief disciples,

sarira are found in the five hundred arhats,

and now,

sarira are found in the dead convicts who cultivated True Buddha Tantra.

Lineage's authenticating objects

I went to pay respect to Guru Tuden Daji in Hong Kong on January 12th, 1993. The visit reminds me of the authenticating objects given to me by the grandmasters of different era.

I list the items below.

Kagyudpa (Red Sect)

1. A small vajra given to me by Liao Ming the monk. The vajra is black, precise, unpolished and has a distinctive sound. The item has been used by Guru Nuo Na.

2. A Manjusri box given to me by Liao Ming the monk. It is a cute and delicate treasure indeed. The item came from Potala monastery. Guru Nuo Na gave the precious box to Liao Ming, who passed to me later. The work is exquisite; it is a very valuable treasure.

Gelugpa (Yellow Sect)

1. A Vajrapani Bodhisattva carved from clay. It belonged to Living Buddha Gan Zhu in the first place. He gave it to Guru Tuden Daji, who in turn present it to me. You can never imagine how

nice this image carved from clay can be. Delicate, solemn and coloured, it is bigger than a thumb but smaller than a palm. It is just marvellous.

2. A Varjayogini carved from clay. It belonged to Living Buddha Gan Zhu originally. The size is the same as Vajrapani. Although uncoloured, it is remarkably true to life. It is inconceivable that Guru Tuden Daji gave it to me.

3. A Golden Time-wheel Vajra. Originally the vajra belonged to Living Buddha Gan Zhu. It is made of pure gold. It has mantra of Time-wheel in front, and the signature of Gan Zhu on its back. Guru Tuden Daji instructed me to wear it whenever I preside over grand ritual.

4. A Diamond dharma wheel- Once it belonged to Guru Tuden Daji. The dharma wheel was made of sparkling diamonds. He told me this is the only one in the whole world- his authenticating token.

5. A gold Vajra and a gold bell- the size of a thumb. They are hooked on to the rosary beads. When I received Supreme Tantra empowerment from Guru Tuden Daji, he gave them to me as tokens.

My lineage gurus from Gelugpa (yellow Sect) gave me a lot of tokens. Gold pin, bat glass, jade elephant, Vajrasattva, crystal ball, double-dragon gold ring, reclining elephant-nose fortune god, just to name a few.

6. A Three-sided Vajra-given to me on January 12, 1993 as token. On top is a three-sided Vajra, below is a single-arm Vajra. Guru Tuden Daji instructed When I hold karma ritual (for confession of sins and absolution) in future, the item can be used to counter all the evil spirits, to turn danger into safety.

Nyingmapa (White Sect)

1. A White crystal rosary beads-the item belonged to the sixteenth Karmapa. He used this hand to hold it and turned the beads. Each bead is as big as a bird egg. It is not the ordinary type. When I received the five Buddha profound empowerment, Karmapa gave me this beautiful rosary beads as a token.

2. A Jade vase-the item also belonged to Karmapa who has all kinds of jade. In fact he has many treasure in his room. The best carpet from Tibet was laid on his dharma seat. He took the jade vase from the pure-white table and gave it to me as a token. The jade vase has been polished, originally it came from Xin Long De Temple, Sikkim.

When the sixteen Karmapa gave me the authenticating object. The lamas in attendance were very surprised. They considered it inconceivable, a magnificent spiritual opportunity.

Sakyapa (Flower Sect)

1. A Sakyamuni Buddha's image-It belonged to Lama Shajia Zhenkong. It is made of brass, quite old and as big as a palm. The item has been with him for a long time. He wrapped it with a piece of white cotton clothes. As he leads an ascetic life, this is one of the few items he carried with him.

2. A Jade lion seal from snowy mountain-It belonged to Lama Shajia Zhenkong, who gave me as a token. Snowy mountain is actually Tang Gu La mountain. The lion from snowy mountain is an intelligent animal. He wanted me to be fearless as a lion from snowy mountain.

Lama Shajia Zhenkong was born in De Gei Bang, Tibet. He became a monk at the age of ten. He left Tibet at twenty six, and has been cultivating in Bhutan, Sikkim and Himalayan area. He observes many strict precepts. Most of my vows to uphold precepts were empowered by him.

Other tokens given by him included lotus flower,

jade pot Vajra head-dress, vajra lock etc.

I am telling all of you my lineage is genuine. A verse written personally by Guru Tuden Daji is on the wall of Rainbow Villa.

The metrical narrative is for Tantra protection,
Climbing mount Lu, I see the bright path.
All sentient beings have the wisdom word-hum,
Its auspicious they follow the right dharma.
The truth will be protected by divine beings,
The dharma favour is extended to all.
The omnipresent truth is accompanied by solemn
    lotus flowers.
Edified by the fragrant incense,
We respect the Buddha's mercy.
Living Buddha Amchok presented me a seat for
    the dharma king.
Living Buddha Shan Shan gave me a robe for the
    dharma king.

This is what I have to say :

Without the wide and profound cultivation, where are the broad and endless virtue coming from?

Without the wide and profound lineage, where are the broad and endless Tantra coming from?

Do think over what I said.

How to become a real True Buddha cultivator A sermon given on Chinese New Year Day 1993

A Building for True Buddha News

I am happy to be able to celebrate this New Year with you. For the past few months, I was rather busy with my propagation. I went to Singapore, Malaysia and Hong Kong last month; and I just returned home last week. To be able to see all of you is like a lady going back to her mother's home. I should say returning to my own home.

I have good news to announce. I have bought a piece of land at Histone Street in the China Town for the construction of a building to be named True Buddha News Building. The first story of which will be an ordinary shop house. The second, an office for True Buddha News. The third, a cultivation place for True Buddha School. The fourth, two units of residence. May be I will migrate to Canada in future.

When the building is put into use, it will make a stir in the China Town. The building will be as long and as wide as that of Bodhi Lei Zhang Temple, which is two storeys tall. The new building will have four storeys. Surely the new one must be better than the old one.

I sincerely hope that True Buddha School will be prosperous, so that we have to find more cultivation centres to cater for the new disciples. If you like to go to Bodhi Lei Zhang Temple, you may do so. On the other hand, if you prefer True Buddha News building, you may also do so. To each his choice, everybody's wish is fulfilled.

The ritual held in Singapore was a success. More than twenty thousand people took part. From Singapore I went to Johor Bahru. The indoor stadium in Johor Bahru has a sitting capacity of eight thousand, exactly the number of people who took part in the ritual. Then it was the ritual held at the capital of Malaysia, Kuala Lumpur's National stadium. Twenty five thousand people attended. The whole stadium was full. Thereafter we travelled to Penang's De Jiao Hui, the ritual attracted eight thousand people. Again we flew from Penang to East Malaysia's Sibu. This time five thousand people came to the ritual. Even in Tawau one of the smallest town in Malaysia with only three streets, we have a Lian Hu Lei Zhang Temple there. The ritual had attracted three thousand people.

The rituals organised by other schools of

Buddhism in Penang at most had an attendance of two thousand, in Tawau four to five hundred only.

Therefore the rituals held in Singapore and Malaysia by the True Buddha School have broken all the local records. Everybody knows that our rituals will surely attract a full crowds. In future, True Buddha School of Buddhism will play a leading role, and enter into the main stream. As a buddhist, a disciple of True Buddha School we must do our part, we must not be too complacent and do whatever we like. On the new year day, I want to talk about how to become a real True Buddha cultivator by doing whatever we have to do.

Observing the five precepts

When Sakyamuni Buddha was alive, he treated his disciples mercifully and equally. Initially he did not ask them to observe any precepts. They could do whatever they liked. The laissez faire led to a degenerated cultivation. The fundamental precepts i.e. the five precepts that Sakyamuni Buddha asked all buddhists to observe, had to be formulated as a result.

The first precept is refrain from killing. All sentient beings are equal. We are sentient beings, so are other animals. Therefore we must refrain from killing them.

The second precept is refrain from taking what is not given. We must observe this precept. We can only consider our belongings ours. Things belonging to others should not be considered and taken as ours. Otherwise, there will be a lot of confusion. In fact, the moral concepts have it that we cannot take other's belongings and claim them to be ours. Just thinking of having them, we have in fact invaded other's right.

The third precept is refrain from telling lies. It looks simple but it is difficult to uphold. We must not tell what is not true. The precept had to be formulated because too many monks were telling untruth, half-truth during Sakyamuni's time. He had to do so.

The fourth precept is refrain from sexual misconduct. Human beings are animals of high intelligence that have morality. In fact, only human beings are capable of doing cultivation. Upholding ethics and moral principles are considered a virtue for a cultivator. In other words, we must refrain from any sexual misconduct. If we do not restrain ourselves and have a strong desire to own, then we are the same as animals.

The last precept is refrain from taking intoxicants.

Once we take excessive liquor, we will misbehave. If you know how to control yourself like me, it will not be harmful. otherwise, it is better not to consume liquor. One cup too many, all kinds of trouble will follow. We know if we drink, we should not drive. Some of us may take advantage of a lady after a drink and regret for life. That is why my advice is not to drink at all. What about smoking ? If Buddha is still alive, I am sure he will not approve of it. Since it is bad for the smoker, and others. The smoke gets in and out of the body, what purpose does it serve ? Normally liquor may have medicinal value to help blood circulation. When taking medicine, we may add a bit of liquor. Don't drink liquor as if you are taking medicine. I have never tried whisky and brandy. I drink only tonics.

The five precepts that all True Buddha cultivators must observe are:

1. Refrain from killing.
2. Refrain from taking what is not given.
3. Refrain from sexual misconduct.
4. Refrain from telling lies.
5. Refrain from taking intoxicants.

As a buddhist, we must always ask ourselves this question, "Are we observing the five precepts ?"

Making a vow and having a merciful mind

After taking refuge, a True Buddha cultivator must make vows (Bodhi heart), Why making vows ? After we get benefits from True Buddha Tantra, we must not keep them as secrets, instead we must recommend them to others. By making vows, we are introducing Tantra to many more people. We can succour as many people as we can. It is important for True Buddha cultivator to remember this point.

So excellent are the True Buddha Tantra that many human beings will be able to gain enlightenment and become a Buddha. After cremation, ten dead convicts from Singapore's Changi prison had sarira found in their remains. These are excellent testimony that they have gained transmigration to the Western Pure Land.

We must make use of the benefits we derived from the Tantra to succour others so that they can be enlightened. The second thing a True Buddha cultivator must do is therefore making vows.

The third pre-requisite, do we have a merciful mind ? If we think of ourselves only in our work, and we never care about others then we do not have a merciful mind yet. When do we consider ourselves to be merciful enough ? -- When we risk ourselves and spend our time for the benefits of others. My

198

vow is "risking my life, breaking my bones to succour sentient beings." In other words, I am willing to sacrifice my life, my time, my energy, and my wealth - everything you name it. This is true mercy, compassion.

People may be risking their lives, breaking their bones in order to make more money, to find happiness for themselves, to achieve their objectives by whatever means in a modern world. As a cultivator, we must not behave like that, we must show our compassion.

Ci, Bei, Xi, She are meaningful words to me.
Ci (kindness) is to bring happiness to all.
Bei(Mercy) is to soothe the pain of others.

We are not tired of bringing happiness to all and soothing their pain is Xi (happiness). What is "Sher" ? For the benefits of others, we dispose of all our belongings is known as "Sher" (abandonment)

The last point I want to talk is cultivating samadhibala. (The ability to overcome all disturbing thoughts -mind control) The five directional Buddhas sitting over there have strong mind control. When we praise them, they do not smile. When we point at their noses and insult their ancestors, they remain unmoved. When a cultivator has attained the

samadhibala, he will show three signs:
1. When you praise him, he will not be wild with joy.
2. When you harm him, he will not feel bad, he is unmoved. No matter how you instigate him, he is not confused- set in an unperturbed mind.
3. No matter how you injure him, his body is non-destructive, and he will never recede in his cultivation. The true samadhibala can only be derived from deep meditation.

Please think for a while.

How good is your mind control ?

If you are scolded, do you go back and think of a sentence more fierce, vicious, and cynical in order to get even ?

If you are insulted, are you able to sleep that night ?

If you are bullied,, are you feeling bad for months even for years ?

To be a real True Buddha cultivator, it is important that you must have samadhibala and have an unshakable confidence - when you hear people taking bad about your Grand master, you must not change your mind and give up to be a True Buddha cultivator.

During Sakyamuni's time, he taught real cultivators the same way:

1. Do you observe the precepts ?
2. Do you make vows ?
3. Do you have mercy ?
4. Do you have samadhibala ?

If you can remember these four points by heart, you are a real True Buddha cultivator.

Talking about how to become a real True Buddha cultivator on a Chinese New Year Day, I hope all of you can be one, not just this year, forever.

I wish all of you

Have good health in the new year, and be prosperous

Om mani padme Hum.

Making Vows

Everyday we cultivate the Amitabha Buddha dharma. We must remember when Amitabha Buddha was in the state of practising the Buddha-religion, as a monk he made forty eight great vows. He only gained enlightenment as Amitabha Buddha when he was in the stage of attainment. The forty eight vows which created the Western Pure Land were only completed after a long time. (many kalpa) His vows can only be fulfilled after such a long time. This shows the greatness of his vows.

In fact all the Buddhas and Bodhisattvas made vows. Amitabha had made forty eight vows, Medicine Buddha had made twelve vows, Avalokitesvara had vowed to use thirty two nirmanakaya to succour sentient beings. After making vows at the initial stage of Bodhisattva, the thousand-arms-thousand-eyes Avalokitesvara Bodhisattva was immediately uplifted to the eight stage of Bodhisattva. We can see the power of his vows. Samantabhadra Bodhisattva had made ten great vows. So was Manjusri Bodhisattva.

A vow is a direction to follow. Every disciple

must make a vow. A true buddhist must find ways and means to fulfil his vow - regardless of the size. Once you have made a vow, you have a direction to go. Can we cultivate without a vow ? A vow is an ideal, an energy source, an ambition, something to go by, that is why all True Buddha disciples must make vows.

Grandmaster's great vow is "Risking my life and breaking my bones to succour sentient beings."

Ksitigarbha's vow- "Unless and until the nether world is empty, I shall not be enlightened as a Buddha." It is a marvellous vow. What does Ksitigarbha rely to become a Bodhisattva ? It is nothing else, just the vow.

Vows are important. We must follow up with our vows. So don't make empty vows. A vow must be fulfilled with all our might. Once a disciple of mine made an empty vow, he said, "My vow is the combined vows of all the Buddhas, Bodhisattvas, Vajra protectors, and Divine beings of ten directions in the three lives." Why not ? Because you do not understand all these vows in the first place. Since you do not understand all these vows how can you fulfil them ? Therefore it will be an empty vow.

Remember, only a vow that can be fulfilled is not an empty vow. The power of vow is very great.

Om mani Padme hum.

The Mantra for making vows

Om Bao Di Zhi Da, Benza, Samaya, Ah Hum.

APPENDIX

APPENDIX ONE

I recalled Xu Yun's poem:
Passing through the "Kong Tong mountain",
Breaking a hole in the cloud, a road passes through,
The meditation room seems far in the evening glows.
The mountain is cold, as the rocks are covered with
    snow,
When the moon touches the heart in meditation, the
five skandhas (aggregates) will be empty. The
stubborn stone blocks the smoke preventing us from
return to the pristine. In the evening, the rain
washes the Kong Tong mountain. The monk cannot
recall what he was asked, as he heard Kuang Zhen
has a wind of Tao.

APPENDIX TWO

I said, "I did not exist in the past, I do not exist in
the present, and I will not exist in the future."
(everything is non-existent.)

Tathgata means "so-come" and "so-gone", i.e. into

Nirvana, so there is "no coming and going."

Since there are "non-birth" and " non-destruction" , the four states of all phenomena (birth, being, change, and death) could not change anything.

Since there is "no coming and going" , the past, present and future lives will not alter anything.

It is said in the "Origin of Human beings",
"Since time immemorial, our body and our mind have followed the law of karma. Like flowing water and burning torch, all of us went through the stages of birth and death without a break. The temporary combination of body and mind was mistakenly viewed as the norm, and fools like us insisted the existence of self."

The truth is very simple, if you know the meaning of "non-self", you will realize everything is non-existent.

Tourl 74
Dreams, Vegetarian and Non-Vegetarian

APPENDIX THREE

About one thousand four hundred years ago, an emperor by the name of Xiao Yan decreed that all monks must eat vegetarian meal only. He was the proponent of vegetarian meal.

This is what I told all the True Buddha disciples:

"Meat has life, so has vegetable. We should not distinguish the different forms of life. Depending on our will, we may be a vegetarian or otherwise. As a True Buddha cultivators, we must visualize, chant and make offering wether we are eating vegetarian or other meal. Tantrayana does not force its followers to be a vegetarian."

APPENDIX FOUR

"Images in the sky" indicated that in future, the youthful True Buddha School will be protected and supported by all the divine beings. With radiating vigor and invincible prowess, it will adopt an unorthodox way of cultivation to succor many sentient beings.

It was a common sight. The moon was hanging in the sky. The bright moonlight was splendid, peaceful and quiet.

But within seconds, it was surrounded by not only one but seven layers of rainbow. The colors of which were magnificent.

It seemed there was somebody in the moon. On second look, it was non other than the picture of Living Buddha Lian Sheng - Master Lu Sheng Yan. Some of the participants even saw the heart Mantra of Living Buddha written on the surface of the moon. They exclaimed and took pride in "Images in the sky."

Why did images appear in the sky? This is a big secret shared by Buddhas, Bohdisattvas and myself. Other people will not know the reason.

Because they did not know the reason they started to use all kinds of words to slander me.

Some of them said solemnly, "Don't tell me, Lu Sheng Yan is really a Buddha, -- the Buddha Light care-free Buddha ?"

The ritual held at Tawau and the resultant "Images in the sky" has made Living Buddha Lian Sheng even more popular. All the newspapers reported such strange occurrence.

Other occurrence may be faked, this incidence definitely cannot be fabricated.

The radiance of True Buddha Tantra is more than a fallen meteorite. It is beyond the moon that sheds light on the dark corners of the earth. It is just like the brilliant sun that shines in high noon.

True Buddha School may appear to be an infant that is still growing, there is no denying that it's Tantra is widespread. Even the most fastidious could not find fault with its Tantra.

The acerbic critics can only resort to personal attack on Lu Sheng Yan. They have not been able to mount any attack on the True Buddha Tantra - a fact that True Buddha School should be proud of.

The phenomona of "Images in the sky" are very difficult if not impossible to explain. It is the flawless and perfect embodiment of divine and Lu Sheng Yan that manifesting in the steps and movement I made.